Discipline

WITHOUT

Punishment

Second Edition

Discipline WITHOUT Punishment

The Proven Strategy That Turns Problem Employees Into Superior Performers

Second Edition

Dick Grote

AMACOM

American Management Association

New York • Atlanta • Brussels • Chicago • Mexico City • San Francisco
Shanghai • Tokyo • Toronto • Washington, D.C.

Special discounts on bulk quantities of AMACOM books are available to corporations, professional associations, and other organizations. For details, contact Special Sales Department, AMACOM, a division of American Management Association, 1601 Broadway, New York, NY 10019.
Tel.: 212-903-8316. Fax: 212-903-8083.
Web Site: www.amacombooks.org

This publication is designed to provide accurate and authoritative information in regard to the subject matter covered. It is sold with the understanding that the publisher is not engaged in rendering legal, accounting, or other professional service. If legal advice or other expert assistance is required, the services of a competent professional person should be sought.

Library of Congress Cataloging-in-Publication Data

Grote, Richard C.
    Discipline without punishment, : the proven strategy that turns problem employees into superior performers / Richard C. Grote.— 2nd ed.
      p. cm.
    Includes bibliographical references and index.
    ISBN-10: 0-8144-7330-X
    ISBN-13: 978-0-8144-7330-6
    1. Labor discipline.   I. Title.
    HF5549.5.L3G76 2006
    658.3'14—dc22

                                           2005025960

Printing number

10 9 8 7 6 5 4 3 2

To Jacqueline
(once again . . .)

In the following pages I offer nothing more than simple facts, plain arguments and common sense; and have no other preliminaries to settle with the reader, other than that he will divest himself of prejudice and prepossession, and suffer his reason and his feelings to determine for themselves; that he will put on, or rather that he will not put off, the true character of a man, and generously enlarge his views beyond the present day.

—Thomas Paine, *Common Sense*

Contents

Discipline WITHOUT Punishment

Second Edition

CHAPTER 1

The Birth of Discipline
Without Punishment

More than thirty years ago I was the manager of training and development for Frito-Lay, one of America's most sophisticated and best managed companies. Out of the blue, we found ourselves ensnared in a public relations nightmare. Day after day, mailbags arrived at Frito-Lay's corporate headquarters filled with angry letters from angry customers. Each letter reported the same bizarre problem: The customer had discovered an obscene message written on a potato chip.

All the chips in question had been produced at the same plant—a plant that in the previous nine months had fired 58 of its 210 employees for various breaches of discipline.

The climate at that plant was toxic. Supervisors there were using the traditional "progressive-discipline" system for all violations, serious or trivial. They eagerly wrote up troublemakers in an attempt to run off malcontents. Every employee who received any disciplinary contact was considered a "troublemaker"; his performance was attentively watched with the goal of finding sufficient evidence of misbehavior to whisk him through the discipline system and out the door.

Of course, with this constant scrutiny, supervisors didn't have much trouble building a case to justify termination.

Employees working in this poisonous environment reacted predictably. All commitment and camaraderie disappeared; employees put forth only a minimum level of exertion. These workers, understandably angry about the constant reprimands, written warnings, suspensions without pay, and terminations, were looking for any way they could find to get even with their hostile and antagonistic supervisors. Eager to retaliate, they found an ingenious tool to get their revenge—a felt-tip pen. One clever individual (we never did discover who he was) found a way to create organizational chaos. He surreptitiously took a chip from the conveyor belt that ran between the production and packaging areas, wrote a vulgar message on it with a felt-tip pen, and returned it to the production line. And he must have told all of his friends about his scheme, since complaints were mounting daily. Faced with dozens of outraged customer complaints, management finally woke up to the need to do something about the disastrous conditions in that plant.

I was given the mission to get into that plant and "shape those knuckleheads up." What I quickly discovered was that the cause of all the disciplinary problems in that plant was the discipline system itself. Our traditional progressive-discipline system, intended to correct poor performance, was, instead, generating it. The long-established approach to discipline—warnings and reprimands and suspensions without pay—produced nothing but belligerence, resentment, and sabotage. In frustration we decided to abandon it, and in its place develop an entirely new approach.

Like traditional approaches, our new approach was progressive: As problems became more serious, our response became more serious. But we abolished all forms of punishment. We scrapped the use of warnings and reprimands and suspensions without pay. Instead, we created a system that focused on insisting that people take personal responsibility for their choices of behavior and conduct—a system that reflected our belief that every one of our employees, even our "troublemakers," was a mature, responsible, and trustworthy adult who would respond that way if we treated him that way.

The most striking demonstration of our total rejection of traditional thinking was our decision to abolish the conventional unpaid disciplinary layoff as the final step. We replaced it with a radical new procedure: a *paid disciplinary suspension.*

Upon reaching the final step of our new "discipline without punishment" system, the individual was told that he must spend the following day at home. He was told to return the day after with a final decision: either to solve the immediate problem and make a total commitment to acceptable performance in every area of his job or to quit and find more satisfying work someplace else. The cost of this day was on the company, we told him, to demonstrate that we were sincere in our desire to see him change and stay. "But if you decide to remain with us," his boss cautioned, "another disciplinary problem will result in your termination." We placed his future in his own hands and told him that we would accept whichever decision he made: Change and stay with us; quit and go find greener pastures elsewhere.

With a great deal of skepticism from many people both in the plant and at corporate headquarters, we installed our new approach. We trained all of our supervisors in the new policy and told the employees that the old ways were gone.

The results? A year later terminations at that plant had dropped from fifty-eight to nineteen; the following year they were down to two. The atmosphere was transformed; the obscene messages, along with the customer complaints, disappeared. Frito-Lay began expanding this "Discipline Without Punishment" system throughout the corporation. Other companies soon followed suit.

Today thousands of organizations have abandoned warnings, reprimands, probations, demotions, unpaid disciplinary suspensions, and all other punitive responses to discipline problems. Some of the results produced at the first group of companies to switch to a responsibility-based approach to discipline were dramatic:

- The Texas Department of Mental Health saw turnover drop from 48.5 percent to 31.3 percent to 18.5 percent in the two years following implementation.

- A Vermont General Electric plant, one of many GE facilities that have adopted it, reported written warnings/reminders dropping from thirty-nine to twenty-three to twelve in a similar two-year period.
- GTE (now Verizon) reduced all grievances by 63 percent and disciplinary grievances by 86 percent in the year after they installed the approach.
- TECO (Tampa Electric Company), one of the first to follow Frito-Lay's lead, reduced sick-leave hours per employee from 66.7 in the year before implementation to 31.2 eight years later. This reduction in sick leave usage resulted in a total savings of $2,662,848 over the eight-year period.

A Better Way

Why do companies still use the antiquated progressive-discipline system? Not because they like its adversarial philosophy. Not because it is required to support a termination if challenged in court or arbitration. Certainly not because of any benefits the system provides. They use traditional progressive discipline because they just haven't discovered a workable alternative—an alternative that is fully accepted by arbitrators and other third parties; one that allows them to confront lapses in organizational discipline in a way that is simple and uncomplicated; and one that enhances the dignity and self-esteem of everyone concerned.

The book that you are holding provides that alternative. The first edition of *Discipline Without Punishment* was published in 1995. Since then, this book has become a minor management classic. It has helped thousands of companies and their managers move to a responsibility-based approach to handling the unavoidable problems of unacceptable performance that come up in every organization, public and private, large and small. In the eleven years since I wrote the original edition I have personally worked with hundreds of companies to help them create Discipline Without Punishment systems that are exactly right for their culture; I have trained their managers to deal with people problems effectively. In that time I have discovered even more effective ways to confront and correct marginal performers. That's the reason I'm writing an updated new edition—so that I can share with you everything I've learned in the past ten years.

This book will help the practicing manager who wants to become better at the toughest job managers face: confronting a subordinate with the need to change. It will also be enormously useful to Human Resources managers who need to make their companies' existing systems more streamlined and defensible. Most of all, however, this book is specifically designed to show all managers, whether line-operating executives or human resource professionals, how to replace their current system with a nonpunitive approach and how to deal with problem performers on the basis of personal responsibility. While the techniques and methods I describe here will certainly help those managers who must use the traditional system to be more effective, my overall position is clear: America's traditional progressive-discipline system does not need to be tuned up or tinkered with. It needs to be abolished.

The Traditional Approach to Discipline

For some seventy-five years, American organizations have been using a standard procedure to handle lapses from organizational discipline. This approach, "progressive discipline," has been concisely described by attorney James R. Redeker in his book *Discipline: Policies and Procedures:*

> The traditional approach, often called progressive or corrective discipline because the purpose is to correct behavior through progressively more severe penalties, has developed into a fairly set formula. This formula consists of a series of steps, one or more of which may be eliminated or added. However, it is rare for the number of steps to be fewer than three or more than five. The following four steps are involved most frequently:
>
> 1. An employee who has committed an infraction is verbally warned and told that if the same infraction occurs again within some specified period the degree of disciplinary action will be increased.

2. If the employee again commits the same or a similar violation within the specified period, the employee will be given a written warning which will be placed in his personnel file. The employee will be told that, if his or her conduct is repeated within a specified period, the employee will be disciplined again but more severely.

3. If the employee again transgresses in the same manner and within the specified period, he or she will be suspended from employment for a specified period of time without pay and will be given a final warning. This warning will clearly specify discharge as the result of another such infraction within the stated time.

4. If the employee again violates the same rule within the specified time, the employee will be discharged.[1]

Figure 1-1 outlines the usual steps of the traditional progressive-discipline system.

Where did this system come from? It wasn't the concoction of management. Actually, the traditional progressive-discipline system was created by unions. In the 1930, unions demanded that companies eliminate summary terminations and instead develop a progressive system of penalties that would provide an employee with a new benefit—protection against losing his job without first being fully aware that his job was at risk. Unions, not management, invented disciplinary action.

Over the years some variations on this progressive-discipline theme have developed, particularly among companies in the nonunion sector. Many organizations feel uncomfortable with suspending someone without pay for a few days, so they eliminate the unpaid disciplinary suspension and replace it with a "probationary period." The employee is told that as a result of his infractions he's being placed on probation for a period of time, most commonly ninety days. He's told that his performance will be monitored closely during this period and if he fails to shape up, he'll be fired.

Other companies choose simply to issue a "final warning" in place of suspension; others demote the individual to a lower rated and less

Figure 1-1. The traditional progressive-discipline system.

INFORMAL TRANSACTIONS

Coaching and Counseling

FORMAL DISCIPLINARY TRANSACTIONS

STEP 1	Oral Warning
STEP 2	Written Warning
STEP 3	Suspension Without Pay/ Final Warning/ Probation
STEP 4	Termination

demanding job. Some companies have even concocted a "virtual suspension," a procedure where the employee is told that she is being placed on suspension and the fact is so recorded in her personnel records, but she is allowed to work during the suspension period and is paid for the time in order not to deprive the individual of pay or deprive the company of her services. Finally, a great many organizations without unions have chosen not to have any formal discipline system at all. Since they operate without the constraints of a union, with its insistence on rigid consistency and the possibility of every adverse action taken with an individual grieved and taken to arbitration, they have chosen not to establish a formal series of steps but instead to deal with problems entirely on an ad-hoc basis. When problems arise in these companies, supervisors engage in whatever "coaching and counseling" attempts they feel comfortable with. The HR department is often called in, either to counsel with the errant employee directly or to provide additional help to the supervisor to bring about a perform-ance change. When the supervisor has finally given up hope of turning the individual around, and the HR representative feels reasonably comfortable that the file of accumulated counseling session summaries and warning letters is sufficiently thick that the termination can with-stand challenge, the individual is terminated.

But the system used in an overwhelming number of organizations, whether codified in policy or simply followed in practice, is the tradi-tional progressive-discipline system that Jim Redeker described. As-suming that the issue being addressed is not so serious that formal disciplinary action or termination would result from a first offense, it calls for the supervisor to engage in informal "coaching and counsel-ing" discussions with an employee and, if these discussions fail to pro-duce a satisfactory change, to begin the formal discipline process.

The Failure of Progressive Discipline

The problems in that original Frito-Lay plant—the miserable morale, the excessive firings, and, finally, the sabotage of our products—caused us to explore not just why the system was failing in that particu-lar plant, but the entire underlying philosophy and assumptions behind it.

The first thing we discovered was that in spite of all the disciplinary action being taken, supervisors were initially reluctant to begin the discipline process. Like their counterparts in almost all organizations, they saw the formal discipline procedure as the mechanism they were required to use to "build a case" against an employee they had de-cided to terminate. Since they saw the system as a means to justify termination rather than to achieve rehabilitation, they often engaged in an excessive number of informal coaching and counseling sessions. Even when the employee did not respond to these informal attempts to bring about a change, supervisors continued these unproductive casual discussions since they hadn't quite made up their minds that the employee was truly hopeless.

When they finally concluded that this individual was not going to make it and that he needed to be fired, they then initiated the discipline procedure with the goal of building a case just as fast as they could. Since they were now determined to terminate the individual, and since they saw the steps of the discipline system as merely the hoops that the personnel department required them to jump through to get there, supervisors became almost blind to any improvements an employee might make.

Our system was failing to meet its most basic responsibility: the development of productive and well-disciplined individuals. Once an individual entered the system, he almost never escaped it. The data were clear: Virtually every employee who received a verbal warning received a written warning; almost everyone who reached the point of a disciplinary suspension was fired not long after.

The problem wasn't the way we were administering the system. The problem was the system itself.

The basic premise of the traditional discipline system is that crime must be followed by punishment. With its constant quest to "make the punishment fit the crime" and its awkward mix of both retribution and rehabilitation, progressive discipline is America's criminal justice system brought into the corporation.

But what do we know for sure about our criminal justice system?

It doesn't work. The traditional progressive-discipline system almost perfectly parallels America's system for handling criminal deviants, and it works no better than the criminal justice system works in transforming lawbreakers into responsible citizens.

Moreover, we realized that our employees were not criminals. They were decent and worthwhile human beings who were always deserving of being treated with dignity and respect. Not all of them had the ability to perform at the high levels that we expected of everyone, whether sweeper or senior manager. Not everyone that we hired had the necessary degree of self-discipline to maintain employment in our demanding industrial environment.

But while some people would fail to meet our standards, either because they were incapable or because they were unwilling, they were not criminals. To use a criminal justice response to their failure to meet our expectations was wrong. We agreed that when a person fell short, we had a responsibility to bring the difference between what was expected and what was delivered to that person's attention and provide him with the guidance and the incentive to meet our goals. We also recognized that, in those few cases where an individual consistently failed to perform to our standards, we had a responsibility to that person's coworkers not to allow him to stay in a job where others were then forced to take up his slack.

But punishment—the warnings, reprimands, and suspensions without pay that constituted our system—wasn't giving us what we needed.

Problems with Punishment

The more we discussed the issue, the more problems we discovered with using punishment as a way to manage and influence people's performance:

• Supervisors often cut some people more slack than others, even though both committed the same offense. If two different employees start arriving for work a few minutes late every day, the manager may immediately confront the issue with the one whose performance in other areas is also deficient. His colleague, with an otherwise unblemished record, is likely to escape with no mention of the lateness problem at all. But word spreads fast, and soon the supervisor is known as one who plays favorites and acts inconsistently.

• Because supervisors may feel uncomfortable taking even clearly appropriate disciplinary action, they often hesitate until there is no alternative. Then, having put up with the employee's misbehavior for so long, they often overreact and confront her far more harshly than the immediate violation might otherwise require. The employee, quite logically, may perceive the supervisor's severe response as a personal attack, particularly since the supervisor has ignored and thereby condoned the earlier instances.

• Over time, punishment loses its power. People get used to it, and, like the heroin addict who must have an always increasing dose, the supervisor must escalate the punishment to bring the same result.

Finally, we confronted the biggest problem of all with punishment:

• While the short-term consequence of punishment is an immediate improvement, the long-term results of punishment are disastrous. Without question, the quickest and simplest way to reduce the frequency of an undesired behavior is to apply some form of punishing consequence. But the reduction in the frequency of misbehavior is the short-term consequence. The use of punishment produces side effects and long-term consequences—anger, apathy, resentment, frustration—that end up being far more costly than whatever the original misbehavior might have been.

We acknowledged the fact that our first-line supervisors faced an almost impossible conflict: On one hand, we asked them to be leaders, teachers, coaches. On the other, we required them to be the dispenser of punishments. No wonder they dawdled and tarried when discipline problems arose.

The New System

We retained the progressive aspect of the traditional approach. But we redesigned all of the steps of the system to eliminate punishment and concentrate on personal responsibility and decision making. Figure 1-2 illustrates the Discipline Without Punishment approach and highlights several ways in which it is significantly different from the traditional progressive-discipline system.

Positive Contacts

To begin, the Discipline Without Punishment approach includes "Positive Contacts" as a formal element of the system. One oddity of traditional approaches to discipline is that they make no provision to recognize the great majority of employees who are already well disciplined. The most frequent complaint of all individuals about their jobs is that they are rarely told when they are performing well. Except per-

Figure 1-2. The Discipline Without Punishment approach.

INFORMAL TRANSACTIONS

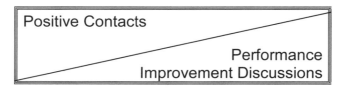

Positive Contacts

Performance
Improvement Discussions

FORMAL DISCIPLINARY
TRANSACTIONS

FIRST	Reminder 1
SECOND	Reminder 2
FINAL	Decision Making Leave

TERMINATION

Termination

haps for the annual performance appraisal, only when problems arise is performance ever discussed.

Including "Positive Contacts" as a formal element of the discipline policy tells managers that recognizing good performance is as important as confronting poor performance. It also makes employees aware that the company expects that they will be recognized when they perform well.

Performance Improvement Discussions

Most supervisors see coaching as part of their ordinary day-in, day-out responsibilities for managing people. These coaching sessions tend to be casual, spur-of-the-moment discussions aimed at showing someone how to do her job better or immediately correcting some minor problem. They are the spontaneous and unstructured problem-solving conversations that happen a dozen times a day. And it's rare for a supervisor to make any written notes of these conversations since they're so brief and unplanned.

Most of the time, these informal discussions achieve their objective. A quick reminder or casual conversation is all that it takes to solve most of the minor problems that come up in any job situation.

But when a problem continues after one of these casual, unrecorded sessions, it's wise to have a more serious, planned-for discussion to let the employee know that immediate change is needed. There needs to be a way for the supervisor to let the individual know that a change is required without having to pull the heavy guns of formal disciplinary action. The traditional progressive-discipline system doesn't give supervisors a useful tool to use when informal chats don't do the job but the supervisor isn't quite ready to move into a formal step of the discipline procedure. A Performance Improvement Discussion is the answer.

Instead of being spontaneous and spur of the moment, a Performance Improvement Discussion requires the supervisor to make notes in advance of the meeting and conduct it with all of the seriousness of a formal disciplinary transaction, but to advise the employee that the matter is still between the two of them. Nothing about the matter will be sent to HR, the supervisor tells the employee—provided the employee solves the problem. If the employee asks if this discussion is a disciplinary step, the answer is no. The purpose of the Performance Improvement Discussion is to avoid the need for any more serious action.

Termination—No Longer the Final Step

Now look again at Figures 1-1 and 1-2. Another major difference between the traditional system and Discipline Without Punishment is the recognition that the discipline process of the latter actually involves only three steps, not four. Termination is not the final step of the discipline system, as the traditional progressive-discipline model would have it. What termination actually represents is not the final step of the discipline system, but the *failure* of the discipline system. The purpose of disciplinary action is to bring about a change in the employee's behavior or performance. Termination is the action the organization takes when disciplinary action fails to produce a change in the individual's behavior sufficient for membership in the organizational family to continue. Portraying termination as the step one takes when disciplinary action has failed makes it easier for supervisors to understand that the time to initiate disciplinary action is when informal discussions have failed to produce a desired change, not when you have made up your mind to fire an employee and view the discipline system as the path to take you there.

A common phrase used by people involved in employee relations is, "Discipline is the capital punishment of organizational life." That's one of the worst descriptions I've ever heard. The appropriate metaphor for termination is not capital punishment, but a no-fault divorce. When disciplinary action fails and termination is required, what the organization is really saying is, "You're a good person; we're a good company. But your needs and our needs are different. We've tried several times to reconcile our differences, and we've failed. You need to find a different job; one that's right for you. And we need to find a different person; someone who's right for us." It's a no-fault divorce.

The Steps of Disciplinary Action

We revised and renamed the "verbal warning" and "written warning"—the first two steps of the approach we had previously been using. Now the first step of disciplinary action has become a *Reminder 1*. Instead of being reprimanded for what he had done, or warned about what would happen the next time he transgressed, the individual is now reminded of two things:

1. *The Company's Expectations.* The supervisor again reviews the performance expectation or job standard that the individual was failing to meet. If the issue is one of attendance, they go over his attendance record and the company's expectation that every employee would show up every day. If the issue deals with a conduct

or behavior issue, the supervisor explains exactly why it is important that the rule he has violated must be followed. If his performance is the issue, the supervisor describes exactly what is expected in quality and quantity of work.

2. *The Employee's Personal Responsibility.* Besides reminding the employee of exactly what performance is expected, the supervisor also reminds the individual of something equally important: that it is he who is responsible for meeting the company's standards. He is told in a friendly and supportive, but also serious and businesslike, way that the company has delivered on its share of the bargain by giving him a good job at excellent pay, together with the tools, training, and support required to do it well. Now he has to live up to his responsibility by actually doing what is expected, and doing it well.

The purpose of the supervisor's discussion is not to deliver a reprimand or warning; instead it is to make sure that the employee fully understands what is expected and that it is his responsibility to deliver.

During the conversation he is told that this conversation is a *Reminder 1*—the first step of the company's formal discipline process (something that had earlier been explained to him and all other employees when the system had been officially installed). He is told that any further problems would lead to the next step of disciplinary action. On the other hand, he is also advised that if he cleans up his act and no further incidents requiring disciplinary action arise within the next six months, this action would be deactivated. His slate could be wiped clean.

The second step of our new procedure we called the *Reminder 2.* It almost exactly paralleled the first step. The supervisor again meets with the individual privately, reviews the situation, and in a serious and businesslike way reminds him once again of both the performance expectation and his responsibility for meeting it. Because the situation has now become more serious, he is told that he will be receiving a memo after the meeting documenting the transaction. While this memo will be placed in his personnel file, he can earn the right to have it deactivated and removed if he goes one year with no further disciplinary problems.

Changing the names of the steps from "oral reprimands" and "written warnings" to *Reminder 1* and *Reminder 2* involves more than mere semantic sleight-of-hand. The changes are substantive, both in the procedures followed and in the discussions that are held. Previously, for example, when a supervisor decided that a written warning disciplinary step was required, he would fill out a preprinted warning notice form, call the employee into the office, hand it to the employee, and say something usually no more gracious than, "Here . . . now what have you got to say for yourself?" The employee at this point felt indicted, tried, and convicted, without ever having been allowed to say a word in his own defense.

After a few moments of sullen silence or acrimonious argument, the supervisor would then tell the employee to shape up and demand that he sign the notice. The employee would refuse, the supervisor would write down that he refused to sign, and then, in an atmosphere filled with animosity and mutual resentment, send him back to work.

(And we wondered why this approach was failing to build a cadre of organization members who were genuinely committed to the company and its goals!)

In instituting the Discipline Without Punishment approach, we had the supervisor begin the transaction not by writing but by talking. We told her to meet with the employee, explain the problem, and then listen to what the employee had to say. After confirming that the issue was genuinely one of failure to meet the company's expectations and not the result of a misunderstanding, the supervisor then would remind the employee of exactly what the company's expectations were and the individual's responsibility to perform as expected. She would then seek to gain the employee's agreement that this would be the last time that the problem would need to be discussed. Upon gaining agreement, the supervisor and the employee would jointly discuss the action that the employee would take to put the problem behind him.

At the end of the conversation the supervisor would advise the individual that because of the seriousness of the situation and their earlier unsuccessful efforts to resolve it, that this transaction was a formal Reminder 2. She would then close the meeting by again reconfirming the employee's commitment that this was the last time they would ever need to talk about the matter.

Following the meeting she would write a memo to the employee, documenting the discussion and the employee's agreement to improve. We believed that using a memo form to document the transaction, rather than a preprinted "turkey ticket" (as employees called it), would cause people to react less negatively to the formal documentation. Writing the memo after the meeting allowed the supervisor to record not only the existence and the history of the problem, but also, much more important, the discussion that they had and the employee's commitment to correct the situation and perform properly in the future.

We looked for any procedures that we could find that would increase the odds that the employee would, in fact, decide to change and correct the problem, without compromising the integrity of the discipline system itself or its ability to support the appropriateness of a termination if challenged. For example, we decided to create a formal mechanism that would allow an individual to deactivate a disciplinary step and get it removed from his file, believing that this would provide a significant incentive for anyone who did get into a disciplinary scrape to clean up his acts. (We also believed that we could deal on an ad-hoc basis with any game-players who tried to tinker with the system by shaping up only enough to get through the guideline period and then repeating their earlier misbehavior.)

In order to give the majority of our people an incentive to change and correct the problem, we consciously accepted the risk that a small number of people might deliberately attempt to manipulate the system and take advantage of us. We were thus operating in exactly the opposite way from most organizations. The approach most companies take is to create systems that provide the greatest possible protection from the minuscule number of employees who are genuinely bad actors and who should be removed from the organization. But in seeking maximum protection as the goal, they often create approaches that are inappropriate for the great majority of their employees. The many must suffer, the organization decides, so that we may protect ourselves against the irresponsible few.

We made the opposite decision. By allowing people the chance to wipe the slate clean, we gave the great majority of employees who are responsible the ability to get an unfortunate incident out of their record. Even for the great bulk of organization members who never create any disciplinary problems, allowing them a "wiping the slate clean" procedure clearly confirms that when the organization speaks of its belief that members of the organization are mature adults who are responsible and trustworthy, it is speaking with sincerity and candor and not with forked tongue.

Decision Making Leave

While the changes we made to the early steps were important, the most remarkable change came in the final step of our new procedure: the *Decision Making Leave*.

In reviewing both our existing procedures and every imaginable alternative, we realized that using a suspension from work as a final disciplinary step had enormous advantages over any other "final step" tactic we could come up with. A suspension allows a cooling off period so that both sides can calmly reflect on the situation. It gives both supervisor and subordinate time to think. By suspending the employee and doing without her services for the period of time she is away, we clearly communicate that we are serious about the matter.

The suspension period is a dramatic gesture. It should force the employee to gain a preview of unemployment, come to her senses, and decide to correct her behavior.

Finally, the use of a suspension gives a company an enormous benefit if an employee is ever terminated and then challenges the action the company has taken. The arbitrator's or judge's or hearing officer's first question will always be, "Did the employee fully understand how serious the situation was? Did he realize that he was in danger of losing his job?" The use of a suspension has universally been accepted by third parties as sufficient notice to the individual that his job is indeed at risk. If he didn't get the message from a suspension, nothing else that the company could have done would have gotten the point across.

A Suspension with Pay?

A suspension from work, we realized, was the ideal final step for any discipline procedure. But when we asked how the company benefits by withholding the individual's pay, we found almost no convincing answers. We knew that the usual employee reaction to the three-day unpaid disciplinary layoff we had been using for years was anger. He left mad; he returned mad. One long-term supervisor commented, "I've never seen a guy come back from an unpaid suspension feeling better about his job or the company . . . or himself."

Taking away the employee's pay brought another party into the equation: the employee's family. Few people who get three days off without pay are unaffected by the income shortfall. They don't have deep pockets. The loss of three days' pay to a family that is struggling to make it on a week-to-week basis means that we're hitting them in the grocery budget. That didn't sit well with the vision we had of ourselves as decent and enlightened employers. Even if we could justify punishing the individual for what he had done, we couldn't accept the idea that it was proper to penalize his family.

After much discussion, we decided that it would be possible to retain the benefits of suspension as a final disciplinary step but eliminate the problems caused by withholding the employee's pay. We devised, as the final step of our new discipline procedure, a disciplinary suspension with pay.

Our final step, the Decision Making Leave, would be a one-day disciplinary suspension. While the employee would be paid for this day, he would be required to use it in both his and the company's best interests. He was told he must use the day off to think about whether he really wanted to work for us. On the day following the suspension, we told him, he must return with a final decision: either to solve the immediate problem and make a commitment to totally acceptable performance in all areas of his job or to decide that working for Frito-Lay was not for him, quit, and go find more suitable employment elsewhere.

We believed we would gain a great many benefits by paying the employee for the day he would be suspended. Our arguments were these:

• *It allows us to demonstrate good faith.* We saw ourselves as decent and enlightened employers; we wanted everything that we did in our employee relations practices to reflect and confirm this view.

Paying the employee for the day allowed us to send the message that when we said we wanted him to use the time seriously to think through whether this was the right job for him, we were sincere. (Suspended employees occasionally commented that they didn't believe that the company would be this fair.)

•   *It transforms anger into guilt.* We knew that virtually every employee who had received an unpaid suspension had been irate; most returned embittered by the experience. But our intent, even with the old system, was not primarily to punish an individual for his transgressions. It was to get him to take responsibility for his own behavior and performance. But docking his pay made our words hollow. Paying the employee, on the other hand, eliminated the anger that commonly resulted from a final step disciplinary transactions.

•   *It eliminates the need to "save face."* We recalled that most employees who returned from an unpaid three-day disciplinary suspension presented themselves as martyrs. They returned to the job with a chip on their shoulder and a need to save face by talking about how good it was to get away from this place for a while. We hoped that by paying employees to make productive use of the time away, we could encourage genuine deliberation and eliminate the desire to "settle the score" on returning.

•   *It makes it easier for the supervisor.* We knew that most supervisors hated having to suspend someone without pay. For the most part our supervisors had themselves come up from the ranks. The employees knew these guys better as peers than as bosses. Their families often knew each other. It was entirely possible that at the same time that a supervisor was holding a disciplinary conversation with one of his workers, their wives were together, playing with their kids. While supervisors may have understood intellectually why the system had to include a suspension without pay, in their guts they hated having to do it. Instead of talking with the individual about the need for change and the company's expectations, they would often apologize to the employee for what they were doing, making an already unpleasant situation worse.

•   *It reduces hostility and the risk of workplace violence.* If anger is generated, the risk of violence grows. We knew that we already had a

serious problem of workplace sabotage on our hands, created by whoever it was who was writing obscenities on chips as they went from
processing to packaging. It was not difficult to imagine that this same
individual, whoever he (or they) might be, could be capable of other
forms of revenge.

•   *It increases defensibility if the employee is later terminated.* Our
decision not to use the layoff period merely as a punishment but instead to require the employee to return with a commitment to fully
acceptable performance would, we believed, increase our chances of
prevailing if we were ever challenged legally later on.

•   *It removes money as an issue.* While the employee is away, we
want him to be thinking about the requirements of his job, his own
occupational goals, and whether the two can be reconciled. Forcing
the employee to worry about how he will make up for the pay he has
lost dilutes the chances that the more important issues will be seriously
considered.

•   *It's consistent with our values.* While it was (and remains) a
tough-minded organization with demanding performance expectations, Frito-Lay was also an organization that took pride in being a
fair employer and a highly desirable place to work. Using a paid suspension and focusing on individual responsibility was a reflection of
senior management values directly on the factory floor.

Making the Move

When our team proposed scuttling the traditional system and changing to a nonpunitive approach, not everyone stood and cheered. Several managers inside the plant and senior executives at the corporate
office had reservations about the possible adverse consequences of this
untested approach. Almost exclusively, their concerns about the system turned out to be unfounded. Among their concerns:

•   *Employees won't take it seriously.* There were fears that employees in the plant would fail to recognize the seriousness of the various
levels of disciplinary action if there was no punishment involved. But

whatever the steps may be, people know what a discipline system is. No misunderstandings arose at all. To make sure that individuals understood the changes and new procedures of our system, we held group meetings with all employees to introduce and explain it.

• *Supervisors won't be able to handle it.* Our supervisors were overwhelmingly relieved with the elimination of the old approach that forced them to be dispensers of punishments. We knew that some supervisors would need more coaching than others in order to incorporate both the mechanics and the underlying philosophy into their day-to-day behavioral repertoire, and we provided it.

There were, of course, some supervisors who resented the change and liked the power the old system gave them to play policeman and write up bad guys. When they continued their old practices they were advised that the old ways were no longer acceptable. Just as they expected their subordinates to adjust to new policies, so did senior management expect that of them. They were told that treating with people with dignity and respect and talking in terms of individual responsibility and decision making are not merely human relations suggestions. They are a condition of employment. Most understood and changed; a few departed.

• *The system won't be upheld by third parties.* While we were operating in a nonunion environment, we knew that employees still had recourse to outside challenge if they felt that they were being dealt with improperly. But we were convinced that our system, even without using punishment, could meet every test of fairness that any jury or arbitrator or other third party could apply.

Our experience in that initial plant, as in the many union and nonunion Frito-Lay facilities that subsequently adopted the system, and in several hundred companies that have installed the system since its original development, is that the Discipline Without Punishment procedure is fully supported as a valid discipline system that fully provides all due process and fairness requirements.

• *Good employees will resent it.* This was a serious concern. Would the great majority of our employees, the ones who never created any disciplinary problems, resent it when their less committed colleagues received a day off with pay?

We tracked that concern carefully and discovered that it was never a serious consideration. As long as they felt that their good performance was recognized and appreciated by the company, the great majority of employees couldn't care less how we handled disciplinary cases, since they were never directly impacted by the system.

We did, however, discover just what it is that good employees do resent. What an organization's excellent performers do take great offense at is a supervisor who discovers an employee who malingers or shirks or evades his responsibilities and chooses to do nothing about it. By creating a discipline system that was more palatable for our weaker supervisors, it encouraged those who in the past might have avoided a disciplinary transaction to confront problems appropriately.

• *People will take advantage of it to get an extra paid day off.* This concern we had no difficulty confronting. On the day we announced the change, several employees facetiously confronted their supervisors with the question, "Hey! Does this mean that if I screw up enough I can get a free day off?" The supervisor laughed and acknowledged that that was indeed the case. "I can get you one right now . . . do you want it?" Of course, no one did. Even the worst organizational game-players quickly realized that there were easier ways to get a "free day off" than by going to the final step of the discipline system.

• *It rewards misbehavior.* This remains one of the most common and deep-seated reservations about the system. Many managers have an ingrained attitude that some form of punishment is the only appropriate response to employee failings in performance and behavior. They think that the failure to respond ruthlessly when someone has acted inappropriately demonstrates a gutless and fainthearted refusal to do what needs to be done. What they fail to see is that requiring someone to take personal responsibility for his own behavior is a far tougher response than merely handing out a punishment.

If the system indeed rewards misbehavior, then we would expect the hundreds of companies that have implemented the approach since it was first developed at Frito-Lay to be reporting an enormous overabundance of misbehavior. They don't. They report the opposite.

Discipline Without Punishment does not reward misbehavior, it confronts it. It confronts misbehavior not merely with punishment which, at best, generates only compliance. It confronts misbehavior with the demand that the errant employee take personal responsibility for what he has done, make a personal decision to either correct the problem or leave the company, and then live up to the decision he has made.

The Results

Between the first of January and the end of September 1973, fifty-eight employees in that Frito-Lay plant were fired for disciplinary reasons. We developed the system in October and November and installed it just before the first of the year. All supervisors were trained, and all employees attended orientation programs. We were frank about the fact that we had problems and needed everyone's help. On January 1, 1974, the new approach went online.

Nine months went by. By October 1, the fifty-eight terminations of the year before had dropped to seventeen. Morale had improved as supervisors abandoned punitive responses and began dealing with problems in a mature and dignified way. Recognition of good performance increased markedly. The atmosphere was no longer toxic. People felt it was now a good place to work. Obscene messages on chips disappeared.

Another year went by. Terminations for the whole year totaled only two. The plant was transformed. Managers in other plants started visiting to see what we had done. They started implementing the approach in their locations and discovered that it worked as well in places where there weren't any problems as it had in our plant. Sales and accounting operations started putting in the system. Other companies had heard about what was going on at Frito-Lay and were calling for information. The word was spreading.

Building Individual Responsibility

In the years since the Discipline Without Punishment approach was first developed at Frito-Lay, hundreds of organizations have adopted it. In almost no other case, however, had companies decided to adopt Discipline Without Punishment in order to overcome the horrendous problems of morale and sabotage such as existed at the plant where it was created. Organizations that implement the system today don't do so because they have lots of problems, but because they don't. They simply find that this approach fits their vision of how an organization that values dignity and respect, individual responsibility, and self-esteem deals with the inevitable problems of organizational life.

America's traditional progressive-discipline system, created in response to union demands, mirrors the values and attitudes of the time in which it emerged seventy-five years ago. This outmoded process—verbal warning, written warning, suspension without pay, termination—reflects the obsolete notion that employees and management are enemies. Progressive discipline is the only vestige of traditional labor-management thinking remaining in most organizations. No other human resource practice has remained in use unchanged since the days of the Great Depression.

But the traditional system is flawed by more than just its exclusive reliance on punishment and its outmoded assumptions about people and work. Its major shortcoming is that it is insufficiently demanding.

To most people punishment seems like a tough way of assuring compliance with organizational standards. If someone fails to meet expectations, we punish that individual until he complies.

But compliance is all that the traditional system can produce, and organizations today need more than mere compliance. While we can punish people into compliance, we cannot punish people into commitment. And genuine commitment to the organization and its goals is what Discipline Without Punishment can produce.

The greatest difficulty with the traditional punitive approach is that it simply asks too little. When an employee receives a warning or reprimand, he is simply scolded for what he has done and threatened with greater reprisals should he choose to continue. No formal commitment to change has been asked or provided. The employee who receives a disciplinary layoff without pay is not required to use that time to consider seriously what he wants out of a job; he is merely asked to serve out his sentence.

But the individual who receives a Reminder 1 or Reminder 2 under the Discipline Without Punishment approach is not punished for the past. He is formally reminded of what the organization expects of him, and, equally as important, reminded that it is his responsibility to meet the company's expectations and do what he is getting paid to do. The individual who is placed on a Decision Making Leave suffers no punishment—he is not docked his pay for the time he is gone; he does not have to dip into savings to keep food on the table while he is suspended from work. But he is faced with a far tougher responsibility than making a few days' financial adjustment because of his loss of a paycheck. He is required to return to work with a commitment: to change and remain part of the family or decide that this is not the right place and move on. He does not merely return to his workstation having simply served out his time. He must stand before his boss and announce the decision he has come to about his own future and his future performance.

The traditional progressive-discipline system takes a problem employee, punishes him, and leaves the organization with a punished problem employee. The Discipline Without Punishment system requires the problem employee to become one of two things: either a good employee or an ex-employee.

Note

1. James R. Redeker, *Discipline: Policies and Procedures* (Washington, D.C.: The Bureau of National Affairs, Inc., 1983).

BUILDING

SUPERIOR

PERFORMANCE

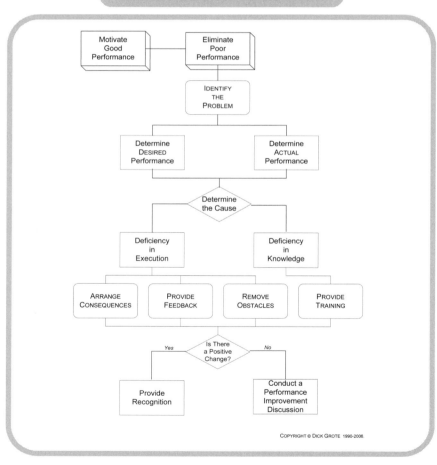

BUILDING SUPERIOR PERFORMANCE

Motivate Good Performance — Eliminate Poor Performance

IDENTIFY THE PROBLEM

Determine DESIRED Performance — Determine ACTUAL Performance

Determine the Cause

Deficiency in Execution — Deficiency in Knowledge

ARRANGE CONSEQUENCES — PROVIDE FEEDBACK — REMOVE OBSTACLES — PROVIDE TRAINING

Is There a Positive Change?
Yes — No

Provide Recognition

Conduct a Performance Improvement Discussion

CHAPTER 2

Recognizing Good Performance

To create a well-disciplined organization, the manager has two primary responsibilities: to recognize and reinforce good performance, and to confront and correct poor performance.

Conducting disciplinary discussions is a very minor part of any manager's performance management efforts. Time spent on recognizing the good performance generated daily by the great majority of organization members will result in far less time spent on problem solving. And problem-solving efforts at the earliest training and coaching stages will result in far less time spent later in disciplinary discussions.

The Discipline Without Punishment system begins by recognizing that the overall objective of the enterprise's discipline system should properly be the development of well-disciplined individuals who are committed to the organization, its mission, its values, and its vision. As a result, the first element of Discipline Without Punishment is Positive Contacts, the recognition of good performance.

Building superior organizational performance begins with the awareness that the great majority of organization members are committed, dedicated, and well-disciplined individuals. While there may occasionally be a need for coaching to enhance a level of performance that is already fully acceptable, or a need for training as new technologies and procedures supplant old, or a need for casual conversations to redirect performance that has gone slightly off track, the manager's primary responsibility in managing performance should be to reinforce the existing level of fully respectable and fitting performance already provided by organization members. In Discipline Without Punishment this recognition of good performance is a formal element of the system—a Positive Contact. The result of using Positive Contacts is the development of motivation.

What Really Motivates People?

What explains human behavior? How can we predict what someone will do? How do we get people to do what we want them to do?

All of us are individuals; no two people are the same. There is, however, one observation about people and their behavior that seems to be true most of the time: *Behavior is a function of its consequences.*

This statement asserts that a person's behavior—the things that a person does and says—is influenced to a large extent by what happens to that person as a result. In simpler terms: "Behavior rewarded is behavior repeated." People do things based on what happens to them as a result.

Psychologists call this idea "positive reinforcement." It works in a straightforward way:

- If a person does something and discovers that the result—the consequence—is *positive* (pleasant, rewarding, desirable), the person is likely to do that thing again.
- If a person does something and discovers that the consequence is *negative* (unpleasant, distasteful, punishing), the person will quickly stop doing that thing.

- And if someone does something and discovers that the consequences are nonexistent—nothing at all happens—that person will
eventually stop doing that thing.

The theory behind positive reinforcement is simple: If a person
does something that we like, she's more likely to keep on doing that
thing if we make sure that there is some positive consequence when
she does it. By reinforcing the behavior, we make it more likely that it
will continue to occur.

Similarly, if a behavior is punished it will disappear—although punishment, as discussed in Chapter 1, generates many additional undesired
consequences. Finally, the person who does something and discovers
that there are no consequences will eventually give up that behavior.

Consequences in the Workplace

In all organizations, the basic principle of "Behavior rewarded is behavior repeated" is constantly at work, whether we're aware of it or
not.

Meetings provide a prime example. Consider why meetings never
seem to start on time. A meeting is called for 9:00 A.M. Those participants who arrive precisely at nine usually feel a little lonely—most
people are late. The chairman then announces, "I see that not everyone's here yet . . . let's wait a few minutes until everybody's arrives."
A few minutes later, when the stragglers finally show up, the meeting
begins.

Consider what just happened. The consequence of coming on
time to the meeting was negative. Those who arrived when they were
supposed to had to wait around, bored and lonely, until the others
showed up. As a result, in the future they probably won't be as concerned with showing up exactly on time.

What was the consequence for those who came late? It was positive: The meeting started as soon as they arrived. Their behavior of
coming late was positively reinforced, so the latecomers are likely to
come to all meetings late from now on.

Here's another example. Let's say that your work group has a major project to get finished, and one of your subordinates volunteers to come in over the weekend to get it done. On Monday morning you find the finished product on your desk.

If you don't say anything to your subordinate, you're providing neither a positive consequence nor a negative consequence. In effect, it's a neutral or "nonexistent consequence." Your subordinate discovers that the behavior of volunteering to work on a project over the weekend produced no consequence at all. How likely is that person to volunteer to work weekends in the future?

Everything that we do in life has some kind of consequence— positive, negative, or nonexistent. Whether we like the idea or not, whether we understand the theory or agree with the concept, it still operates to influence performance.

When people perform well, the effective manager looks for ways to reinforce good performance, rather than allowing things to happen by chance or at random. A skillful manager makes sure that employees discover that there are positive consequences for maintaining good attendance records, doing jobs well, following safety procedures, offering suggestions for improvement, and all of the other day-to-day things that too often are ignored or go unnoticed.

Reinforcing Good Performance

In virtually every organization the level of performance provided by organization members will form the familiar bell-shaped curve. While the overall performance level of some companies will be higher than that of others, as will the performance of some departments within a company be better than that of others, within one organization or one department we will almost always find that there is pretty close to a standard distribution of performance. At one end of the curve there will be a small number of people whose performance is outstanding or distinguished—in gardening terms, your organization's roses. At the other end will be another small number whose performance is unacceptable—the weeds. And in the middle will be the great majority of individuals, some of whom will be performing better than others, and all of whom will fall between the two extremes of distinguished and unacceptable. They are the good solid citizens of your corporate garden—your daisies.

Ask the typical manager which of these three groups he spends a lot of time with, and the answer is immediate: the weeds. These are the problem children who demand his attention; these are squeaky wheels to which he must apply some managerial grease.

Then ask if there is another group which commands his attention. Of course—the roses, the pool of exceptional performers.

What happens, then, to the daisies, the great majority of people who are somewhere in the middle? They're ignored. In most organizations, day-to-day management attention is directed at those who perform in ways other than competently, diligently, and at a fully satisfactory level. The manager's attention is commandeered by those that inhabit the ends of the curve. The vast majority, the daisies who make up the middle of the organization's garden, are unseen.

But organization members who perform somewhere in the middle form the backbone of the enterprise. Ignore them and we eliminate the incentive for them to do any better than they are right now. The message we send to them seems to be: Want managerial attention? Move to one end of the curve or the other. And since becoming a rose is extremely difficult and probably beyond the capability of most organization members, the easy way to get managerial attention is to slide downwards toward the weedy end of the performance curve.

Our greatest opportunity for increasing overall organizational performance lies with our solid, competent performers. The sluggards, misfits, and organizational ne'er-do-wells at the bottom end of the curve must be confronted and either turned around or replaced. The whiz kids and virtuosos at the high end must be rewarded (and usually are). But the overall performance of any organization cannot be significantly influenced by action taken with either of these two groups, simply because the population in each is too small to make a critical difference. But if each individual in the huge population of middle-ground performers increases his or her contribution by just 10 percent, the impact on the entire organization will be enormous. And the best way to spur performance improvement is to make sure that we provide a positive consequence—*recognition*—whenever it happens.

When Is Recognition Appropriate?

There are three situations where recognition of good performance is appropriate. First, when an individual has done something "above and beyond the call of duty." Most managers are able to identify when a person has performed in a truly exceptional way and recognize the outstanding performance appropriately.

The second situation worthy of recognition involves those cases in which an employee has significantly improved his or her performance, either after a coaching or disciplinary transaction, or simply by the individual's personal efforts to move to a higher level of contribution. Again, most managers are sensitive to these situations and know that reinforcing the improvement will provide an incentive to continue.

The most difficult situations to recognize are those where the employee hasn't done anything particularly special or outstanding. The individual has simply met all of the organization's expectations over a long period of time.

In this third case, the need for performance recognition is more difficult to identify since the person has neither performed in a truly outstanding manner nor has corrected a significant problem. Instead, the individual has simply maintained an ongoing record of competent, proficient, and sustained performance over time. Since the person is doing exactly what we expect, it is easy to overlook the need for recognition.

An easy way to visualize the three varieties of performance described above is to consider the attendance records of three different employees over the period of one year. The first individual was able to maintain a perfect attendance record. During the entire year there was not one scheduled work day when this person was late or absent. Most managers realize that this level of outstanding performance needs to be recognized if it is to continue.

The second individual did not have a perfect record. In fact, this person's record was exactly average. The year before, however, he had compiled the company's worst attendance record and was told that he must correct his absence record or face discharge. He did what it took and is now at the "fully acceptable" level. Again, most managers will agree that providing recognition for this improvement will help sustain the correction.

The third individual had neither a perfect record nor a previous problem. Instead, over the course of the year she had missed only one day of work (when the company average was four incidents of absence per employee) and had reported late to work only twice (again, while not perfect, much better than average). Is this individual likely to receive any form of personal recognition for her far-above-average performance?

In most companies, no. Most managers would agree that her record is certainly one to be proud of, but the likelihood is slim that her boss will call her in to his office and say, "Sally, in going over last year's attendance records I noticed that yours was well above average. It wasn't perfect, but that's not the important thing. I know that there must have been times when you had to make a special effort or a personal sacrifice in order to be here, and I want you to know that I genuinely appreciate that."

Since those words are never said, the message that the employee does receive is, "Nobody noticed . . . nobody cares." People in organizations listen as loud to what we don't say as to what we do, and our unspoken, silent messages communicate as clearly as any verbalized pronouncement. As a result, the next time she awakens with a nasty dose of hemorrhoids and heartburn, indisposed and uncomfortable but still capable of reporting for duty if she had to, she will likely roll over and say, "Why should I bother . . . they don't care."

Our challenge is to find examples of good performance to recognize. Somewhere between the parameters of barely acceptable and genuinely heroic are hundreds of people who are simply doing their jobs just a little better than they have to. If we actively seek out this level of performance, we will discover an abundance of it.

Identifying Behavior to Recognize

In my seminars I always ask the managers to generate several examples of an employee who is performing properly. No matter how much I stress the importance of being specific, their initial responses are all broad generalizations. "Someone who's diligent and reliable," they tell me, or "someone who takes initiative," or "somebody with a good attitude."

It is as important to be specific when we are recognizing good performance as it is when we are trying to bring about a performance correction, I explain. If we cannot tell employees exactly what it is that causes us to feel good about their performance, the odds are slim that they will be able to continue that good performance. They won't know exactly what it is that they did to bring about our approbation.

"What would you accept as evidence of a good attitude?" I ask them. "Give me an example of taking initiative." The manager who suggests "taking initiative" as an example of good performance has to expend some effort to translate that general description into the far more precise statement, "someone who finishes the patient record updates that she has been assigned and asks her coworker if she needs help in completing her stack."

With just a bit of coaching, most managers are able to translate their initial generalizations into specific observations of measurable behavior. Here's the test for determining whether your description of an individual's performance is sufficiently specific—can you make a snapshot or movie or tape recording of it? If you can, it's specific. If you can't, it's not. You can't take a snapshot of a good attitude; you can easily make a tape recording of someone saying, "Here, let me give you a hand with that."

When managers narrow their description of an individual's performance to actions and behaviors that are specific and precise, they often feel that the behavior they are describing seems somewhat small—even insignificant. But superior job performance is not a matter of doing a few things heroically. It is instead a matter of doing a great many small things well. If the manager provides recognition for small stuff, the big deals will take care of themselves.

Guidelines for Effective Recognition

The single most important guideline for using Positive Contacts as a tool to influence good performance is: *Do it often.*

But in addition to frequency, there are other considerations to make recognition of good performance effective. Performance recognition works most effectively when it is swift. A common mistake managers make when they encounter an example of good performance on a subordinate's part is to delay holding a Positive Contact discussion until the annual performance appraisal. Not only are the details and nuances of what was done often forgotten, the event itself may be forgotten over the passage of several months. Positive Contacts are most influential when they rapidly follow the behavior being reinforced.

Performance recognition is also most effective when it is directed to specific individuals, rather than to teams or groups of employees. While the team as a whole may have achieved a goal, individual members of the team may have contributed at varying levels. Make sure that the distinctive contributions of various individuals on the team are acknowledged as well as the success of the team as a whole.

Tailoring is another important criterion for Positive Contacts. What one person sees as a reward may be viewed by another as a punishment. Some people like to have their contributions made known to the group directly; others prefer that their achievements be acknowledged privately.

Finally, all recognition of performance needs to be proportionate. Both the sincerity and good sense of a manager who praises a minor contribution lavishly are questioned by the recipient of the accolade and by others. Balance is vital; fulsome praise for minor achievements is invariably spurned.

"Think small" is a cardinal rule in using positive consequences to influence performance. Don't wait until a person has performed perfectly to provide recognition. Acknowledge the minor achievements that produced the ultimate result.

Recognition Tools

Managers have many tools at their disposal to use in arranging for positive consequences for good performance. Here are a dozen items that managers have reported using with a high degree of success to recognize and reinforce the good performance of a subordinate:

- Assign the individual to work on a more desirable job.
- Give her an advance copy of a new company brochure or advertisement.
- Buy her a cup of coffee.
- Introduce him to a visitor and explain to the visitor how his work contributes to the success of the department as a whole.
- Write her a memo commending a job well done and send a copy to her personnel file.
- Write a quick "Thanks!" on a Post-It Note and stick it on her phone when she's away from her desk.
- Write your boss a memo about what the employee accomplished and send a copy to the individual.
- Ask his advice about a business-related matter—how to reduce waste, how to improve customer service, how to reorganize the work flow when a fellow employee is away on maternity leave.
- Arrange for her to be given a supply of her own business cards.
- Let him take an extended lunch.
- Clip an article of interest from the newspaper and pass it along.
- Make a ridiculous plaque and conduct a silly presentation ceremony.

All of these can be powerful reinforcers of good performance and, used wisely, will have the effect of significantly increasing the frequency of an individual's engaging in the actions or behaviors that have been reinforced. But of all these, the most important are the sincere and genuine words that come out of our mouths: "Well done," "Thanks," or "I genuinely appreciate that."

Our words are the most important tool we have to influence the performance of others. Simply telling a subordinate that we have noticed and appreciate the individual's good performance in one area of her job increases the probability that the good performance will continue.

For example, General Electric's aircraft engine plant in Rutland, Vermont, implemented its nonpunitive discipline procedure a number of years ago. A year after implementation I returned to the plant to do a refresher training program with a group of managers in the plant. In our discussion about recognizing good performance, one of them, the plant's maintenance manager, related an experience he had had.

About two months before, as he told the group, one of his mechanics had quickly fixed a nasty machine malfunction that threatened to shut down production. That night he and his wife were in a grocery store. He was telling her about what the guy had done. As they passed the magazine rack, he picked up a skiing magazine to give to the mechanic, since he knew the guy was a ski nut.

The next day the manager spotted the mechanic and pulled him into an empty cubicle. He explained that at the grocery store the night before he had told his wife about what he had done and then handed him the ski magazine as a way of saying thanks.

He said that the mechanic just stood there, all choked up and wordless. "Hey, it's just a ski magazine," said the manager, uncomfortable with the mechanic's emotion. The guy shook his head and struggled to say, "You told your wife . . . ?"

"Yeah, I told her what you had done and got you a ski magazine to say thanks."

"You told . . . your wife . . . about me?"

That's when the light went on for him, the maintenance manager told the group.

"Yes," he said to the mechanic. "I told my wife what you had done and how proud I was of you."

At that point the machine operator, holding back tears, ran out of the cubicle, clutching the irrelevant ski magazine.

"Let me tell you what I learned from that," the maintenance manager told the group. "I learned that this mechanic had just discovered something he never knew. He discovered that I didn't look at him like he was some kind of Martian who comes down from Mars at 7:00 in the morning and goes back up to Mars at 3:30 in the afternoon. He discovered that I knew he really existed, and that I would tell my wife about him. That's when I really understood what's important about recognition. It's not the programs, the ski magazines, the trinkets, the employee-of-the-month crap. It's the words that come out of my mouth: 'Thank you,' 'Good job,' 'I'm proud of you,' 'I told my wife about you . . . .' "

The Dark Side of Recognition

Recognizing good performance—arranging positive consequences to increase the frequency of desired behavior—is not a way of being nice to one's workers and increasing one's popularity. It is a practical, tough-minded, and demanding management tool to influence people's behavior on the job.

Ask any group of supervisors if discrimination is illegal and they will all instantaneously agree that it is. They're wrong, of course.

Discrimination on the basis of some things—race, religion, handicap, age, sex, etc.—is illegal and should be. It doesn't correlate with performance. But discrimination on the basis of performance is not only legal, it is mandatory if an organization is going to be able to prevail in a tough competitive environment. Even organizations that appear to be removed from the pressures of competition—a city government, for example—may not have to compete for customers, but still must compete to attract the highest quality employees and keep them from being lured by other employers.

Using positive consequences and providing recognition of good performance requires that managers discriminate against some employees in favor of others. They must discriminate—not on the basis of race or sex, but on the basis of performance—and make sure that only those who have earned recognition receive it.

In my seminars I always ask participants—once we have reviewed the importance of recognizing good performance and identified all of the tools available to managers to reinforce desired behavior—why managers don't do more of it. "There's probably not a person in this room who has been told by his boss too often that he's doing a good job," I tell them. "We are all living in a state of stroke-deprivation."

"Why don't we do it?" I ask.

Their answers are almost always predictable:

"We're too busy."

"We don't notice ordinary good performance since it's what we expect."

"Nobody does it to me."

"I feel awkward telling someone he's done a good job."

And while all of these responses, excuses, and explanations are understandable and believable, they miss the subtle but most authentic reason why we don't use recognition to motivate improved performance. Recognizing good performance forces us to discriminate among our people—to separate those who are performing well from those who are not.

To use positive reinforcement effectively, we must not only provide it actively to those whose performance justifies our providing it, but we must also consciously withhold it from those whose performance does not justify their receipt of extended lunches and Post-It Notes and more desirable job assignments and managerial applause. Managers have no difficulty agreeing that positive consequences should be provided to those whose performance qualifies them for it. They have enormous difficulty accepting the corollary of that statement: that the intangible rewards of organizational life should consciously be withheld from those who have yet to earn them.

The Treat-Everybody-Alike Manager

Consider a manager who makes the following statement and think about whether this approach appeals to you:

> I am a manager who never plays favorites. As a boss, I would never do for one of my people what I wouldn't do for all. We're a team here, and I make sure that everyone on the team is treated alike.

That statement has an enormous seductive appeal to most people. They like the sound of it. But examine the effect of that approach to managing people and you discover that the manager who makes that statement is actually saying that he treats the people who contribute the least to his organization the same way that he treats those who contribute the most. He plays no favorites. No special rewards are provided to those who carry more than their load.

There are some employees who love working for a manager with that philosophy. Who are these people? The weeds—the ones who are at the lower end of the performance curve. And what do they do when they discover that they're working for a manager or for a company that isn't willing to do anything for the best employees that they won't do for everybody else? They get on the phone and call all their weedy little friends, saying, "Come on down to Acme Industries! They're hiring people just like us!"

There are others who loathe that approach to management—the roses. These are the people who perform at the highest end of the curve. They quickly discover that their exemplary performance provides no benefit. Do well, do poorly—you're treated the same.

These star performers move. Some move on down the performance curve to a spot just above the middle; comfortably at the "slightly above average" level. There they can turn on their occupational cruise control and coast comfortably. Others, with too much personal pride and self-respect to coast, and frustrated because their exceptional performance is ignored by the manager, quit. They ask themselves, "If my boss doesn't care about excellence, why should I?" They find it easy to leave and find another organization where exemplary performance is rewarded.

The manager who takes pride in "treating everybody alike" will probably never be caught or confronted. He will simply drift along, content with the mediocre performance that his department or unit or function is producing. He will never be accused of discriminating or playing favorites. From time to time he may observe that many of his better people seem to be leaving. Occasionally he will notice that people who yesterday seemed to be highly committed and motivated now seem to have lost some of their spark and drive. But he will never have to explain to one subordinate why another subordinate is being treated better.

* * *

The manager who works to encourage outstanding performance from his people has chosen a stonier path. On those who excel, he showers all the discretionary organizational rewards at his disposal, and he finds many. But to those in his work group who fail to perform at those high levels, he deliberately and consciously withholds those rewards. All mandatory benefits are provided, of course. Those whose performance is at the bottom of the curve receive every organizational goodie to which they are entitled and continue to receive them up until the day they are fired. But the extended lunch hours, the more desirable assignments—the appointment to special committees and task forces, the little congratulatory Post-It Notes that others receive—are denied them.

And what do these people do when they realize that the discretionary rewards the manager has to dispense are not distributed equally? They complain, of course. They gripe about favoritism; they whine about discrimination.

But the manager who has chosen this more arduous path, the manager who believes that good performance is worthy of reward and, concurrently, believes that mediocrity should be slighted and rewards withheld, has the courage to confront the whiners and gripers with the acknowledgement that they are correct.

"You are right," he responds to the complaint that Sally got an advance copy of the new brochure and Charlie was asked to show the chairman around and Suzie got first choice of furniture, and you didn't do anything like that for me. "I didn't, and I chose not to do so consciously and deliberately."

"The reason I didn't," that intrepid and forthright manager continues, "is because you haven't given me the right. I wish I could do for you what I have done for them, but you haven't given me any justification. But let me tell you this—the instant that your performance is at the same level as Sally's and Suzie's and Charlie's, I'll be there with the same rewards for you that I've given to them. It's your decision."

In 1997, Roberto Goizueta, the then chairman and CEO of the Coca-Cola Company, died. Goizueta had started with Coke at the bottom and worked his way up to the CEO's job. An immigrant from Cuba, he became one of America's most successful business leaders. When Goizueta died, the *Dallas Morning News* not only carried his obituary, the newspaper also wrote an editorial celebrating his remarkable career.

The editorial described what an astute and far-sighted business executive Goizueta had been. But the editorial concluded with this powerful observation about the man: "In judging those who worked for him, Mr. Goizueta was free of every prejudice, except one. He favored employees who produced results."

Our ability to discriminate determines whether we will be successful in our efforts to manage performance. If we have the courage to reward abundantly the good performance that the majority of our people provide, and withhold those rewards from those few whose efforts do not justify providing them, we will have a wholly motivated enterprise.

Solving People Problems

For an organization to enjoy universal high performance, it must recognize the good performance delivered by the great majority of organization members. The more that the manager provides positive consequences (Positive Contacts) for good performance, the more likely it is that good performance will be delivered.

In spite of any action that managers take, however, people problems will still arise. When they do, managers need to confront the problems and make sure that the individual's performance returns to a fully acceptable level.

Some performance problems can easily be defined in a specific and measurable way. In the area of attendance, for example, the employee's variation from organizational expectations is clear and visible. The company expects the employee to be at work every day on time; in the last three weeks Henry has arrived at work more than twenty minutes late on three separate occasions. In this case both the desired and the actual performance are clear.

In other cases the gap between desired and actual is more difficult to define. When the concern is related to the quality of an individual's work, or to her relations with customers and coworkers, or to his general demeanor and attitude, it is more difficult to develop a straightforward description of the variance between what is expected and what is delivered. But whatever the issue may be, problems can not be solved until they can be identified specifically.

Types of Problems

To begin, it is useful to recognize that all problems of human performance in an organization fall neatly into one of three categories: attendance, performance, and conduct:

1. *Attendance.* Attendance problems arise when an individual fails to meet the company's expectation that she will be at work on time every day. When a large health-care organization recently implemented Discipline Without Punishment, they articulated their attendance expectations in a way that could not be misunderstood. Their policy states: "Our attendance expectations are simple and clear. We expect every employee to be at work, on time, for the full duration of the scheduled work shift, every day that the employee is scheduled to work."

2. *Performance.* These issues involve problems with the quality and quantity of the individual's work. Issues in the performance category include such things as failure to meet deadlines, failure to attain goals, excessive scrap and waste, provoking customer complaints, or wasting time.

3. *Behavior/Conduct.* The behavior or conduct category involves those issues that deal with violating the organization's rules or standards. Examples would include smoking in a restricted area, inappropriate use of company vehicles, failure to comply with expense reimbursement procedures, safety violations, unauthorized acceptance of gifts, and theft of company property.

Sorting a problem into its appropriate category is helpful for two reasons. First, these three categories describe the universe of possible problems the manager may encounter. Any problem that arises in an organization will be either an issue of attendance, of performance, or of conduct. It is helpful, therefore, to start the problem-solving process by narrowing down the specific category into which the specific concern falls.

Second, it is helpful to note that the three categories of performance problems are mutually exclusive. In other words, not only do all performance problems that the manager will ever encounter fall very neatly into one of the three categories, but there is no overlap between the three. The employee who has a problem arriving for work on time every day (a problem in the attendance category) may do an excellent job while he's there and never violate any of the organization's rules. Another individual may smoke in a restricted area (a conduct issue) but perform at a highly competent level and maintain an excellent attendance record. Or there is the person whose quality of work is unacceptable (a performance concern) but who maintains an acceptable attendance record and follows all the company's rules and standards.

Wait a minute—managers frequently respond once they've encountered the idea that all problems fall in an orderly way into the three uncluttered categories of attendance, performance, and conduct—what about somebody with an attitude problem? Which category is that? Or is that a separate category all its own?

No, it's not. Attitude is a behavioral issue, so consider it to be in the behavior/conduct category. But attitude problems are a bit of a sticky wicket. We deal with attitude problems in detail when we get to Chapter 9.

Segregating problems into one of the three categories will be particularly useful later on when we explore how to administer a discipline system. One of the most difficult issues managers confront is figuring out when a disciplinary step should be repeated and when it's appropriate to move to the next more formal level. How many Reminder 1s can an employee get? When should that individual move to the Reminder 2 stage? If the organization tags problems as attendance, performance, or conduct issues, it becomes much simpler to provide workable guidelines on the number of disciplinary transactions an individual may receive.

Making Problem Definitions Specific

Problems in the attendance and behavior/conduct categories are fairly easy to describe in terms of the specific difference between desired and actual performance. You want all employees to be at work, ready to go, at 8:00 A.M. In the last four weeks there were three occasions when George didn't arrive until 8:15 A.M. You want all machine operators to wear safety goggles any time they're using a lathe; Harriet was running the lathe without safety goggles on. The gap between desired and actual performance is clear in both cases.

That's not always true when the issue is one of performance—quality and quantity of work. Some of these cases are fairly straightforward: Managers are expected to get all performance appraisals written and submitted to their bosses for review by April 27; it's now May 4 and three managers have yet to complete their appraisals. The difference between what you want and what you get is obvious.

But other performance issues aren't as clear. Our tendency is to generalize about problems. While our generalizations may be accurate, they're not helpful in getting employees to understand the exact gap between desired performance and their actual performance.

In a seminar at a large hospital in the Southwest, the director of the dietary department began the problem identification process by describing an individual who wasn't a team player. "What makes you say that?" I asked her.

"He doesn't show any team spirit," she responded.

The whole seminar group and I then analyzed what had just happened. To support one generalization—"He's not a team player"—she had simply offered up another—"He doesn't show any team spirit."

"Let me try a different approach," I responded, once she and the others saw how common it is to try to support one judgment or generalization by offering up another. "If you had to prove in court that this person truly wasn't a team player, what could you offer as evidence?"

I divided the group in half. I asked the dietary director and her teammates to come up with a list of the actual things that an individual might do that would be acceptable evidence that the person really did have a problem with working effectively as a team member. The other half of the group I set to work generating a list of actions that they would accept as specific evidence that an individual was indeed a team player.

Their results:

- *Actual Performance* (evidence that someone was not a team player):
    - Works on obviously low-priority job tasks when she could be assisting others with much more important parts of the job.
    - Wanders in other areas with no valid reason.
    - Does only those tasks that are specifically assigned.
    - Says, "That's not my job," when asked to take charge of an unusual situation.
    - Makes negative comments about the quality of others' suggestions (for example, "That's a dopey idea . . .").
    - Makes negative personal comments about other people (for example, "What doofus here is trying to say is . . ." when a fellow worker got tongue-tied during a team meeting).
    - Makes no effort to get along with others, as shown by sitting alone in the cafeteria at lunch and not participating in group social activities.
    - Says, "I don't need anyone's help," when the manager asks a fellow employee to work with her on a minor project.
- *Desired Performance* (evidence that someone is a team player):
    - Demonstrates a spirit of cooperation as shown by not monopolizing time during a team meeting.
    - Offers up solutions to team problems and not just complaints about their existence.

- Supports coworkers' ideas and suggestions by saying things like, "That's a good idea, Mary."
- Offers to assist others in their duties when time is available.
- Supports coworkers by making positive statements about them and asking if they need help.
- Asks coworkers for assistance in her projects to demonstrate that others are also members of the team.
- Assists others when they ask for help, or politely explains why she can't at that time.

The best way to overcome the temptation to generalize or be judgmental about problems is to ask the question, "What do I know for sure?"

Determining the Cause

Once we have clearly identified the specific gap between desired and actual performance, the next step is to determine why the employee isn't doing the job properly right now.

When a person isn't performing the way we expect, there are only two causes. The performance deficiency involves either a lack of knowledge or a lack of execution. Either he doesn't know how to do the job right, or he does know how to do it right but something is getting in the way. The easiest way to determine the actual cause is to ask the question, "Could he do the job properly if his life depended on it?"

If the answer is "No"—no matter how hard he tried or how motivated he might be, he couldn't do the job right—then we're probably looking at a problem caused by a deficiency in knowledge. The individual doesn't have the knowledge or skills required to do the job right, and some kind of training is probably required.

But if the answer is "Yes"—he could do the job properly if he had to, but he still isn't performing properly—then we're dealing with a deficiency in execution. In this case, the employee has the knowledge and skills required to do the job properly, but isn't executing.

It's important to distinguish between knowledge and execution problems because the solutions will be very different. Training is the obvious solution to a knowledge problem, but training won't help when the cause of the problem is a lack of execution.

When discussing performance deficiencies on their subordinate's part, managers often make the mistake of describing them as "training problems." If we define performance problems as training problems, we are confusing the cause of the problem with its solution. We are committing the same error as the individual who goes to the doctor with a headache and explains, "Doc, I've got an aspirin problem." He doesn't have an aspirin problem . . . he's got a headache. Aspirin may be a solution. Antibiotics may be a solution. Brain surgery may be a solution. But his problem isn't aspirin—the problem is, his head hurts. The manager doesn't have a training problem, he has a performance deficiency.

Training may occasionally be the solution to performance problems. But based on my experience of working with thousands of managers, it rarely is. Hundreds of times I have asked managers to make lists of the specific performance problems they face. They write down the things their subordinates are doing that need to be changed. We refine them into detailed and measurable statements of desired behavior and actual behavior.

Once they have written their statements in terms that are specific and unarguable, I ask them to determine whether each of the problems that they have identified are knowledge issues or execution issues. Is this one caused by a lack of knowledge and skill, or is this situation one where the individual could be performing properly if he had to, but isn't?

The results are always the same. Out of two dozen problems the group has listed, perhaps one or two will be caused by a deficiency in knowledge. Another two or three may represent a combination of the two. But by far the great majority are issues where the deficiency is one of execution. The individual could be doing the job right if he had to. He does know how, they tell me, but he isn't executing.

Recognize the limitations of training. To be blunt, the only thing that training can predictably do is provide knowledge and skills where they don't already exist. As valuable as this may be, most of the time it takes something other than training to solve the performance problems managers face.

Solving Execution Problems

Deficiencies in knowledge are cured by training. What do you do when the person knows how to perform properly, but still isn't doing the job right?

These are the cases where managers are particularly inclined to blame the employee's bad attitude or complain that he just doesn't care. While in some cases it may turn out that the individual truly does not care, usually the problem results from something interfering with proper performance. The need here is not for training; it is for job engineering. Three solutions are available to put things right: Remove obstacles, provide feedback, and arrange appropriate consequences.

Removing Obstacles

We can only expect people to perform their jobs well if they have all the resources required to do the job properly. If a person does not have the equipment needed to do a job or receives conflicting instructions, or if a bad environment or poor working conditions interfere with job performance, the employee will be unable to do the job right.

Job interferences are frequently difficult to identify since we may be so used to going around them that we don't even notice that they exist. It is often useful simply to ask if there's anything that gets in people's way as they try to perform successfully.

In today's business environment, no organization is able to provide all of the resources that would enable every employee to do his job without interferences. Limited resources are, and will continue to be, a fact of life. Too often, however, the obstacles that interfere with job performance are ones that could be easily eliminated if the manager actively seeks to help her employees perform well.

Providing Feedback

A recent survey reported that fully 80 percent of American men believe that they are in the top 10 percent of athletic ability for their age group. In the absence of accurate feedback, people tend to believe that they are better than they truly are.

Regular, accurate, and timely information is one of the most important tools for any individual to use in maintaining acceptable job performance.

The classic application of using performance feedback to improve job performance involved Emery Air Freight's success in increasing the use of containers to consolidate several small packages into one large container. The company's stated goal was 95 percent utilization of containers and, while it was not precisely measured, the assumption on the part of most managers and employees was that the 95 percent goal was being achieved regularly.

One day an Emery senior manager actually audited the operation to see what percentage of shipments that could be containerized actually were containerized. He was astounded at the result. Instead of 95 percent, it was 45 percent.

The problem was corrected by providing feedback to each individual dock worker about his actual level of performance. This was done with a form that required the dock worker to write the name of the shipper for each item, to note whether each package being processed met the requirements to be containerized, and to indicate whether it actually was containerized. At the end of the shift the dock worker calculated the actual percentage of those containerized against those that should have been containerized, and turned the form over to his foreman. The foreman calculated the percentage and posted the results for everyone to see. When this form was introduced nationwide, the overnight result was an increase in containerization from a national average of 45 percent to 95 percent.

Arranging Appropriate Consequences

When people are punished for doing their jobs well, or rewarded for doing them poorly, or discover that it makes no difference how well or poorly they perform, problems invariably result.

Several years ago I was asked by United Airlines' director of reservations, Ted Hattan, to create a training program for the company's experienced reservations agents. We met in his office to talk about what he wanted the program to accomplish.

The problem, he explained, was not at all one of courtesy or customer service. They regularly monitored calls and knew that the agents, almost without exception, were doing an excellent job of providing information and booking flights. The difficulty, Hattan explained, was that they weren't selling. "A secretary calls and tells the agent that her boss and three of his people are planning to fly next Wednesday from Washington to San Francisco and asks what time our flights leave. That's a perfect selling situation. But all the agent does is tell her what times our flights to San Francisco leave then thanks her for calling and hangs up. No effort to sell at all . . . a blown opportunity. I need for you to teach them to sell!"

Before beginning work on an advanced selling-skills program, I asked Hattan to let me talk to some of the agents and supervisors. It didn't take long to discover that a training program would have been worthless.

United's reservations office was a huge room on the second floor of the hangar. Over 250 agents sat in rows, each one wired to her phone and computer. High on the wall, about fifteen inches across, was a red light that looked like a giant taillight from an ugly 1950s sedan. Whenever customers were calling and the office was so busy that the calls went into the holding queue, the red light would flash like a monstrous turn signal. The supervisors would then scurry up and down the aisles, whispering to the agents, "Take more calls . . . we're holding calls . . . take more calls!" The agents would then simply provide information and abandon any attempt to sell.

A second problem emerged. Ask an agent how he or she was doing as far as sales were concerned, the response would be, "Just fine." Everyone knew that the office stressed selling, but nobody had any specific information on their actual sales. They all thought that if there were problems with insufficient selling, somebody else wasn't trying hard enough. They had no information on their own actual performance.

Finally I discovered the biggest problem of all. While Ted Hattan and his managers talked constantly about the importance of selling, the only data they measured and fed back to the agents were "calls per hour." Calls-per-hour was the measurement used to evaluate performance when appraisal time came around; calls-per-hour determined the amount of an agent's merit increase. When that secretary called in asking about flight times, the sophisticated agent would graciously provide the times and quickly say, "Thank you for calling United." Hey, a call's a call.

The solution to Ted Hattan's problem was simple, cheap, and elegant. One third of the agents were shown how to tap the computer to find out exactly what their sales for the day or week had been and how they compared to the office average. They were told to stay with a sales opportunity even when the call-holding light was flashing. And they were told that while calls-per-hour was important, turning nibbles into actual seats booked was much more important, and that their performance appraisals would reflect both measures. They were also given a refresher training session on how to convert inquiries into seats sold.

Another third of the office got the same adjustment—computer feedback, rearranged consequences—but no training. The final third of the office was a control group. They experienced no changes in their jobs and didn't participate in the training program.

The results were both predictable and surprising. It was predictable that the first two groups would far outperform the third, and they did. What was surprising was that there was no significant difference between the improved performance of the group that got feedback, consequences, and training and the other group that received only the job engineering changes. Both increased sales about 24 percent. The other surprise was that there was very little reduction on either of the "experimental groups" in their calls-per-hour. Agents monitored their conversations carefully, responding to informational calls quickly and sticking with nibbles until the sale was made.

The truth is, few performance problems are caused by an employee's lack of knowledge or skill. Training is the answer to deficiencies in knowledge, but when reasonably experienced performers fail to perform properly, a lack of knowledge is rarely the cause.

Some are caused by position mismatches: the square peg in the round hole. Neither training, nor job engineering, nor disciplinary action can cure these situations. Transfer if possible, downgrade to a position the person can handle if not. Terminate if all else fails.

The solution to a great many performance deficiencies, however, lies in re-engineering the job. Arrange for people to get feedback so that they know exactly how well or poorly they are doing, remove any obstacles that thwart good performance, and rearrange the consequences so that performing well makes a difference.

Shifting the Responsibility from Manager to Employee

When a supervisor appeals to his boss or the human resources department for authority to take disciplinary action or terminate an employee, it's common for the response to be, "Have you done everything that you needed to do?" While it's easy to ask this question, it's rare that the HR rep or senior manager is able to specify exactly what it is that the supervisor is responsible for doing.

There are five—and only five—things that a supervisor is responsible for doing before he can legitimately say, "I have done everything I am responsible for doing." These five things are to clearly specify the exact gap between desired performance and the employee's actual performance, provide whatever training is available to develop the needed knowledge and skills, remove any obstacles that prevent the individual from performing properly, provide feedback so the individual knows exactly how well he or she is doing, and arrange appropriate consequences so that the person doesn't find himself punished for doing a good job or rewarded for performing poorly. For each these items I have listed below two questions to ask to be sure that management's responsibilities have been met:

- *Clarify expectations.*
  - Can the individual explain exactly what is expected?
  - Does the individual understand the exact gap between desired performance and actual performance?

- *Provide training.*
  - Does the employee have the knowledge and skills needed to do the job?
  - Has the individual received the same training as other people?
- *Arrange appropriate consequences.*
  - What happens to the individual:
    1) when he performs properly?
    2) when he does not perform properly?
  - Does doing the job properly or quickly produce unpleasant consequences?
- *Provide feedback.*
  - How does the individual know exactly what's expected?
  - How does the employee know exactly how well or how poorly he's doing?
- *Remove obstacles.*
  - Does the person receive any conflicting messages or instructions?
  - Does the employee have the time, the tools, the equipment, the authority, and the support needed to do the job?

Once the manager has asked and answered these questions, he has done everything that he is responsible for. The burden for solving the problem now shifts to the employee. No longer will the manager, the night before he fires a subordinate, have to grapple with the question, "Is there anything else I could have done?"

The answer to that question is *no*. There are things that the manager and the organization must do before saying that the responsibility for correcting the situation now lies entirely with the individual. The manager must make sure that the job, by a normal person with normal training, can be done as expected. The manager must make sure that the employee has had the training needed to perform properly. The manager must be sure that the employee knows exactly what the company's expectations are and how he's doing against them. Finally, within the limits of organizational realities and constraints, the manager must make sure that no problems with obstacles, feedback, or inappropriate consequences prevent the person from doing the job right.

But once the manager can state that the employee knows exactly what is expected; that she is recognized appropriately when she performs as expected; that she knows how to do the job properly, encounters no obstacles, and knows exactly how well or how poorly she is doing, the manager has done all that he can reasonably be asked to do. It is at this point that the burden of responsibility shifts from the organization to the employee. The individual with the problem now becomes the one who is fully responsible for its solution.

PERFORMANCE

IMPROVEMENT

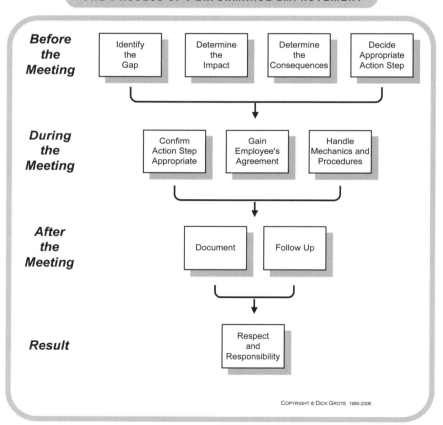

THE PROCESS OF PERFORMANCE IMPROVEMENT

Before the Meeting

Identify the Gap

Determine the Impact

Determine the Consequences

Decide Appropriate Action Step

During the Meeting

Confirm Action Step Appropriate

Gain Employee's Agreement

Handle Mechanics and Procedures

After the Meeting

Document

Follow Up

Result

Respect and Responsibility

COPYRIGHT © DICK GROTE 1990-2006

CHAPTER 4

Preparing for a Performance Improvement Discussion

Most people do their jobs well. The job performance of most employees never falls below "acceptable" and is usually significantly better.

When performance problems initially arise, the effective manager starts by determining the most likely cause. Is it a knowledge problem for which some form of training would be appropriate? Or is it an execution problem where the issues of feedback, obstacles, and consequences should be explored?

This problem-identification process does not happen in a vacuum. Good managers are always talking with their people, doing the constant reviewing and discussing that causes problems to become visible early when they can be easily solved. Determining the cause of a subordinate's failure to meet expectations is not something that the manager does analytically in the privacy of his office. He does it by informally and casually talking with the individual whose performance is the source of concern.

But too often managers avoid this straightforward and direct approach. They're reluctant to discuss performance problems with subordinates. They don't know what to say. They're uncomfortable with their lack of skill and fear the harm that may be done to an otherwise effective working relationship. So they wait until one of two things happens. First, the problem may go away on its own. While certainly this happens from time to time, the problem is equally likely to return, since it was never actually addressed and corrected but simply allowed to wither and die. When it arises again it will now be even more diffi-cult to solve since the manager, having ignored the situation origi-nally, is now seen as having sanctioned the previous misbehavior.

The other possibility is that the problem will continue to grow to the point where it cannot be ignored and must be confronted. But by now it is a more difficult situation. The problem behavior has become rooted and habitual, and the manager, having said nothing earlier, is now a virtual coconspirator in the misbehavior. "Why did you wait till now?" the employee complains when he is called on the carpet. "Why didn't you tell me a long time ago?" The complaint is valid.

Before moving into disciplinary action, it's important for supervi-sors to discuss the need for performance improvement so that prob-lems get solved without having to move into the formal discipline system. (Of course, there are those problems that are so serious that it's appropriate to deal them with a formal step of disciplinary action or even termination for a first offense. We discuss these types of situa-tions and how to handle them in Chapter 10. But for now, let's recog-nize that the overwhelming majority of problems that supervisors encounter are the less serious misdemeanors for which a discussion about the need to improve performance is more appropriate than a formal disciplinary transaction.)

What Is a Performance Improvement Discussion?

The process of solving people problems so that problems are elimi-nated and relationships are enhanced begins with a Performance Im-provement Discussion.

A "Performance Improvement Discussion" is not a spur-of-the-moment event. It is a serious and planned discussion between a manager and an employee about the need to correct a problem and improve performance. It has specific goals and follows a definite structure. Unlike spontaneous casual discussions about problems, a Performance Improvement Discussion always involves careful planning in advance.

One of the great benefits of providing for Performance Improvement Discussions as a regular part of a discipline process is that it provides a needed bridge between the informality of casual conversations about performance issues and the often rigid formality of the official discipline transaction. Holding a Performance Improvement Discussion with an employee allows the supervisor to communicate the urgency of change at the same level of seriousness as she would in one of the formal steps of disciplinary action, but without the sometimes burdensome administrative requirements of approvals and documentation and witnesses and other impediments.

It is useful to distinguish among three kinds of discussions supervisors can hold with subordinates: casual conversations, Performance Improvement Discussions, and disciplinary transactions. Most managers assume that casual conversations and Performance Improvement Discussions are very much alike, and that disciplinary transactions are significantly different.

That's not the case. Under the Discipline Without Punishment system, Performance Improvement Discussions and disciplinary transactions are almost indistinguishable. The only significant difference between a Performance Improvement Discussion and a step of disciplinary action is that in a disciplinary transaction, the supervisor advises the employee that the discussion they are having is a formal level of the Discipline Without Punishment system, and then documents the discussion following the conversation.

Other than that, they're the same thing. The procedures that the supervisor follows for an effective Performance Improvement Discussion are the same as those of an effective disciplinary conversation. He identifies the specific problem that needs to be solved, analyzes why a change must be made, discusses it with the employee to gain the individual's agreement, makes a note about what they have discussed, and follows up to make sure the problem has been corrected. The appropriate tone is calm, dignified, respectful, business-like, and professional, whether the discussion is a Performance Improvement Discussion or a Decision Making Leave.

Conducting the Performance Improvement Discussion

As the diagram at the beginning of this part of the book illustrates, a Performance Improvement Discussion involves three components: what the manager does before the meeting to prepare for the face-to-face session; what she does during the meeting; and what she does when the meeting is over and the employee returns to work. The result of following this process is that you build respect for yourself as a manager, respect for the organization and its standards, and individual responsibility on the employee's part. And while I'll be talking about the things that the manager does before, during, and after the meeting in the context of the Performance Improvement Discussion, the fact is that these same steps apply whether the transaction with the employee ends up being a Performance Improvement Discussion or a formal step of disciplinary action.

This chapter covers the first component: the manager's pre-meeting preparation. There are four things a manager needs to do to be fully prepared to talk with a member of her team about the need for a performance change:

1. Identify the specific difference between actual and desired performance.
2. Analyze the impact of the problem—the good business reasons why it must be solved.
3. Identify the consequences the employee will face if change doesn't happen.
4. Determine the appropriate action step.

In Chapter 5, "Conducting the Performance Improvement Discussion," I tell you exactly about the second component: how to hold a discussion about the need for a change in performance. Whether the discussion is one of the formal levels of Discipline Without Punishment or a Performance Improvement Discussion, the structure and procedures of the face-to-face discussion will be the same.

The third component of a Performance Improvement Discussion, the things the manager is responsible for once the discussion with the employee has been completed, basically involves documenting the discussion and following up to make sure that the problem has been solved. These responsibilities are covered fully in Chapter 6, "The Mechanics of Discipline Without Punishment," and Chapter 7, "Decision Making Leave."

Identifying the Gap

As I described in Chapter 3, any performance or behavior problem can be separated into one of three categories: attendance, performance, and conduct.

Start by determining which of the three types of problems is the primary concern. While an individual may have a need for improvement in several areas (an unacceptable attendance record may be combined with a failure to submit scheduled progress reports on time), keeping unrelated issues separated increases the chances of getting each problem solved. Moreover, if the discussion is a formal disciplinary transaction, the procedural aspects of the discipline system will be easier to manage when every disciplinary discussion focuses only on one of the three problem categories.

In other words: Got two problems? Hold two discussions.

At early stages, when the probability of correction and commitment are highest, there is no absolute prohibition against talking about several performance concerns in the course of an informal discussion about performance. But when concerns about performance have grown to the point where the manager has decided to schedule a specific meeting with the subordinate to discuss the need for change, restricting the discussion to the top-priority issue will increase the odds that the subordinate will agree to change and return to fully acceptable performance. Dumping a gunnysack of problems will suggest to the individual that the real issue is not his own poor performance but some personal failing on the manager's part. The subordinate will discount all of the unconnected deficiencies about which the manager is complaining as merely additional proof of the manager's tendency to nitpick and relieve pressure by taking out his frustrations on his subordinates. Quick and unconvincing agreement will probably be forthcoming, as the subordinate, eager to get the meeting over with and get back to the job at hand, simply concurs and harmonizes with whatever the boss puts forth.

Managers can increase their effectiveness by starting a meeting with a multitroubled subordinate by saying, "Jack, there are probably a number of things that we should be talking about. In the last few weeks I've expressed my concern at various times about the number of customer contacts you're making, about your reluctance to get involved with the trade association to make new contacts, even about your being away from your desk too often to catch a smoke. But those things are really secondary. Today I want to concentrate on talking about one key issue with you. That is, your total sales have fallen by 16 percent in the last three months. . . ."

Now the subordinate knows that while all those other infractions have not been forgotten, they are secondary. The manager can concentrate on the most significant issue and then, once agreement to solve the critical problem has been gained, can mention the need for a total commitment to acceptable performance as the meeting is wrapping up.

It's usually a fairly easy matter to determine the category into which a problem falls. Being specific about desired and actual performance is much more difficult.

Determining Actual and Desired Performance

Instead of concentrating on the precise change needed in the subordinate's performance, most managers tend to talk in vague and general terms. Since the manager himself has not taken the time to determine exactly what acceptable performance is—and what it is not—it is almost impossible for the subordinate to know exactly what is expected.

Why is it so important to be so specific? Consider what happens in a restaurant when we experience an evening of enjoyable food but wretched service. To communicate our unhappiness with the waiter's service, we leave a nickel tip. When the waiter discovers our paltry tip, our unhappiness will instantly be communicated. But in the absence of any data about the cause of our unhappiness, the waiter's immediate assumption will be that the problem resides, not with the service he provided, but with us as the customer.

Consider all the explanations the waiter is likely to come up with to explain the insulting tip:

- The customer made a mistake—the tiny tip was inadvertent.
- There was something wrong with the food.
- There was something wrong with the restaurant—too warm, too cold, too smoky.
- The customer had run out of money and left everything that he had.

In each case, the waiter's explanation of the lousy tip acknowledged the fact that a problem existed, but denied the possibility that he himself was the cause. The waiter will tell himself that whatever the reason may have been for the meager tip, it certainly had nothing to do with poor service.

The same situation happens in organizations when managers fail to be specific about the problem and the resolution required. If the manager only communicates a general feeling of unhappiness, the subordinate will understand that the manager is upset. But the subordinate will explain away the manager's unhappiness in the same way the waiter did:

- He's picking on me because his boss chewed him out this morning.
- She's disappointed she didn't get appointed to the steering committee.

- He must have had a fight with his wife.
- It must be her time of the month.
- She's one day away from vacation and she's just trying to get us all to work hard while she's gone.
- He just doesn't like us elderly, black, female, Spanish-surnamed, handicapped homosexuals.

To solve problems effectively we must be able to describe what it is that we *want* and what it is that we *get* in the individual's performance. It is the subordinate's responsibility to close the gap between desired and actual performance. Our responsibility is to specify exactly what the gap is.

For some problems, it's easy. Problems that fall into the attendance category are the easiest to identify specifically, because the gap between desired and actual performance is always clear: "Between June 16 and July 23, Jane Edmondson was absent from work on three occasions for a total of five days. In that same period she reported to work late by more than ten minutes on two separate occasions."

Note that the problem statement says nothing about the cause of Jane's absence. It does not say that Jane was ill or called in sick or abused her sick-leave privileges or did anything other than simply fail to report to work every day on time. That is all that the manager knows for sure. The cause of Jane's absences may be considered at some other more appropriate time. But at this point, when our only task is to identify the difference between desired and actual performance, we restrict ourselves to writing down the answers to two straightforward questions:

1. What is the desired performance? (What do I want?)
2. What is the actual performance? (What do I get?)

Here are some examples of various problems stated in terms of actual and desired performance:

Desired Performance   Employees are to smoke only in designated smoking areas or outside the building.

Actual Performance	George Adamson was seen smoking in the cafeteria.
Desired Performance	Upon being given an instruction by any member of management, employees are to perform the task assigned. If they believe that the manager giving the instruction is in error, they are to complete the task assigned and then question the appropriateness of the assignment.
Actual Performance	Upon being told by the department manager to stop what she was doing and assist two other employees finish a complicated customer order, Julie Sonnenberg stated, "You're not my boss. You can't tell me what to do." She continued to work at the task she had been assigned by her immediate supervisor earlier.
Desired Performance	All drivers are expected to operate their vehicles courteously.
Actual Performance	On May 17 a woman called the 800 number posted on the back of company trucks to complain about the erratic driving and speeding of a company truck that was being driven at the time by Danny Di Sabatino.
Desired Performance	All nurses are expected to respond to any patient call button within three minutes on the 11 P.M. to 7 A.M. shift.
Actual Performance	On the evening of March 16, patient Claudia Gonzales complained to the day nurse that the night nurse hadn't responded to her call button the night before.
Desired Performance	All employees of the corporation are prohibited from engaging in any unwanted or inappropriate behavior of a sexual nature, whether physical, verbal, nonverbal, or any other type, expressed toward any employee, customer, applicant, vendor, supplier, or other individual having a relationship with the organization.
Actual Performance	On September 5, Joe McKenna approached Sharon Peterman at the copy machine and said, "You sure make that sweater look good." When Peterman turned away without responding, McKenna said, "The package sure is pretty . . . I'd sure like to get my hands on the contents."

In each of the preceding cases, there are several common factors. While the problems themselves are completely unrelated, the statements of desired and actual performance are clear and unambiguous. Not one contains any statement that involves a judgment by the manager or a generalization based on the facts. Instead, the statement simply provides a clear description of the variance between what was expected and what was delivered.

The statements, in other words, are written to be *unarguable*. The individual certainly may protest that he really had good reasons for failing to meet the performance expectation, or may say that the seriousness of the action is being exaggerated, or may argue that failing to meet the expectation is not a serious matter. While these issues may be worth discussing, there is no argument that the actual description of the employee's behavior is accurate. Adamson was, in fact, observed smoking. Mrs. Gonzales did, in fact, complain about a delay in getting a response to her call button. Julie Sonnenberg did, in fact, refuse to follow the department manager's instruction.

Note also that there is no indication of the seriousness of the problem in any of the statements. In these five examples we have illustrations of five unrelated problems that can arise in any organization. The least serious may be George Adamson's decision to smoke in the cafeteria. A word in George's ear will probably snuff out that situation forever.

More serious is the example of the night nurse's failure to respond to a patient call button. The statement of desired performance expresses a clearly defined performance expectation: respond to all call buttons within three minutes. Failure to meet the standard may result in an extremely serious consequence (if the patient was calling because of a life-threatening incident) or may be completely trivial (if the reason for the call was the patient's desired for a kind word and a back rub). But the effects of her failure to perform is not our concern yet. The issue at this stage in the process is to describe exactly what the desired performance is and exactly how the individual failed to meet that requirement.

George Adamson's smoking problem may be dealt with simply by saying, "Come on, George . . . you know you can't light up here."

The more serious problem with the nurse's failure to respond to a call button require anything from a casual and informal reminder (if the patient is a known crank), to a very serious disciplinary transaction (if the nurse consciously ignored the summons, and the safety of the patient was compromised). Finally, the sexual harassment charge, if proved, could even result in the termination of the harasser, based on the complete set of facts that will emerge during the investigation. But at this point, our sole objective is to identify precisely what the variance is between what we want and what we get.

Avoiding Assumptions

In none of the preceding descriptions of actual and desired performance are there any assumptions, or characterizations, or attitudinal allegations. In the most serious example, the situation involving an apparent sexual harassment case involving Joe McKenna and Sharon Peterman, the description of desired performance is simply the corporation's published policy regarding sexual harassment. In the description of actual performance, the statement does not say that McKenna "harassed" Peterman. There are no characterizations of his behavior as "leering" or "ogling." It does not say that he made his statements "suggestively" or "lewdly" or "in a vulgar manner." It does not claim that he was "obscene" or "vulgar" or "carnal" or "lascivious" or "lecherous," since these would be conclusions drawn on the basis of what was actually done.

In addition, since they speak to McKenna's presumed intent or purpose, they would be very hard to support if challenged. Instead, the statement simply describes exactly what he said and did without embellishment. He walked up to her in this place, spoke these words, and when she turned away without responding, spoke these additional words. The statement is not only unambiguous, it is unarguable.

In this case, McKenna may argue that his remarks were misinterpreted. He may claim that this was part of an ongoing relationship they had and that he assumed that they would be taken in the light and playful manner he intended them. He may present all kinds of arguments in his defense, but the unarguable fact is that these were the words that he spoke. That is what we know for sure.

Determining the Facts

What do you know for sure? In preparing for a Performance Improvement Discussion with an employee, this is the single most important question you can ask. You do not know that McKenna harassed Peterman. It sounds like a blatant example of sexual harassment, and later it may be determined that it is. At this point, however, all we know for sure is that he spoke these words and she complained about it.

We do not know for sure whether the night nurse had a good reason for not meeting the three minute standard for responding to call buttons. She may have been involved in a critical care situation on a different part of the floor. We do not know for sure whether Julie Sonnenberg may have justification for not following the department head's instructions. We do know for sure that she refused.

The point is not to turn managers into prosecuting attorneys, but to force managers to restrict themselves to dealing only with information that no plaintiff's attorney could twist and use against the manager later. By restricting ourselves only to what we know for sure, we will be far more comfortable when we talk to the employee about the need to change. We accuse the employee of nothing. We make no assumptions about the individual's intentions or motives. We cast no aspersions on the truthfulness of any statements the employee makes in his or her defense. We are simply saying, "Here is what we expect, and here is what actually happened. There is a difference, and this difference must be corrected."

This approach makes it easier for managers to confront problems when their information is secondhand. In two of the preceding examples—the situations with the night nurse and the truck driver who was reported to be driving erratically and speeding—neither the individual's direct supervisor nor any other member of management observed the inappropriate behavior. Managers are often reluctant to confront this kind of problem, anticipating that the employee's reaction will be, "How do you know what I did? You weren't there!"

In these cases, dealing exclusively with what the manager knows for sure allows him to confront the problem more confidently and more accurately. In the case of the nurse, the nursing supervisor can comfortably respond to the employee's rebuttal that she wasn't there by saying, "Barbara, you're right. I wasn't there and therefore I don't know all the details of what happened and why. What I do know is that when I came in to work this morning I received a complaint from a very upset patient who told me that she had rung her call button twice during the night. Once, she said, there had been no response. Half an hour later she said that she rang the button again and you showed up about ten minutes after that. I don't know whether she is correct or not. What I do know is that I got a serious complaint, and that's what we need to talk about. How do you need to manage your response to call buttons so that we never get any complaints?"

Likewise, in the driving situation, it is far easier to deal with the situation and get a problem solved (if, in fact, a problem actually does exist) if the manager acknowledges up front what the employee already knows and is eager to point out—that the manager was not there and therefore has no firsthand data about the way in which the employee was driving his truck. But that is not the issue, the manager can explain to the individual. "Granted," the manager can say to Danny, "it is conceivable that the woman who called to complain about your driving is a nut case. She sounded entirely reasonable and rational on the phone when I talked to her, but it is possible that she may be deranged. But that doesn't address the issue that someone who observed your driving was sufficiently concerned to take the time to call the company to bring it to our attention. That is all we know for sure, and that is what we need to talk about. What do you need to do in the future, Danny, to make sure that your driving never provokes people into feeling that they need to call us about it?"

Danny, the driver, may well to come back with a rejoinder about being unfairly accused, arguing that he is invariably a model driver. But his boss is in a strong position to press for a commitment for a performance change, based not on the supposition that Danny's driving was excessively fast and erratic (which it probably was but the manager does not know for sure), but on the fact that, whatever his driving demeanor was, it was of such a nature that it caused someone to call and complain.

"I'm not asking you to slow down and drive safely," Danny's boss can tell him, "because you have told me that you already are and I believe that you are telling me the truth. What I am asking for is your agreement that, whatever it takes, you will drive in such a manner that no one ever feels the need to call us and complain."

When the manager has identified the problem in terms of the specific difference between actual and desired performance so that the description is unarguable, only the first part of the manager's premeeting preparation has been completed. He knows the category the problem falls into and he knows the exact difference between desired performance and actual.

But the manager is not yet ready to initiate a discussion. Merely being aware of the existence of a problem is insufficient ammunition to generate a commitment to change. There are still three more elements of preparation. Now that we know exactly what the problem is, we must also be prepared to explain why it must be solved, what the consequences will be if it's not, and what kind of discussion we're going to have with the individual about the need for change.

The Purpose of the Discussion

When a manager and a subordinate sit down to talk about a problem, what is the manager's goal for that conversation?

The easy and obvious answer is, of course, to get the problem solved. And while solving the problem is the long-term goal, the actual correction will not occur until some point in the future, long after the meeting is over. The question we are raising here is a more tightly focused one: What needs to happen while the meeting is going on to tell the manager that she can say, "Ahhhhhhh, I have achieved my goal. Now I can wrap this conversation up and we can get back to work."?

What is your goal *during the meeting itself*? What needs to happen while you and the subordinate are talking to tell you that you can now bring things to a close because you have accomplished your objective?

It has nothing to do with the manager's feelings about whether the subordinate has sufficiently internalized the necessity for change or fully comprehended the gravity of the situation. It is far, far simpler.

The goal of the meeting is to get the subordinate to agree to change.

That's it. Period.

"Well, that's simple," most managers respond. "I knew that."

I would then counter with a second question: Why is it so important to get the employee to agree to change?

The obvious answer is that if he says he'll change then he probably will. Certainly the individual who agrees to change is more likely to actually change and get back to fulfilling the requirements of the job than is the person who is simply ordered to. But there is a more subtle and more powerful reason.

Have you ever experienced roller coaster performance? Have you ever had someone working for you who had some performance problems and got better for a while after you talked to him but then reverted back to the unacceptable level after a while? And you'd talk again and he'd get better for a while and then he'd slough off again? And you'd talk again and the cycle would continue: talk, get better, get worse; talk, get better, get worse.

Most managers are familiar with that scenario.

Here's the antidote. The reason that the goal of the conversation is to get the employee to agree to change is not only because the person who agrees to change is more likely to change. The other, more important, reason is this: If the person agrees to correct a problem and then later the same problem arises again, the manager will hold another conversation with the individual. But the subject of this second conversation will be different than that of the first. This time the subject will be the employee's failure to live up to the agreement.

In this second conversation, the manager might say something like this: "George, a week or so ago we talked about the need for you to smoke only in the prescribed areas or outside. You agreed that you would do so. This morning I noticed that you were again smoking in the cafeteria. But I'm less concerned about your continuing to smoke in a restricted area than I am about your decision not to live up to your agreement. That's the real issue now. Tell me, George, how can we maintain an employment relationship with someone who decides not to live up to an agreement that he makes with his boss?"

Now *there* is a question worth asking.

Gaining the employee's agreement serves two important purposes. First, if the manager is successful in getting the individual to agree to perform at the level of expected performance, the odds go up that the individual will, in fact, live up to the agreement that he has made.

But the second reason is the manager's ace in the hole. If the misconduct or unacceptable performance continues, the subsequent conversation will focus not just on the continuation of the original problem, but on the employee's failure to live up to the agreement.

Gaining Agreement

How do we gain a person's agreement?

The work we did in identifying the specific difference between actual and desired performance makes the process of gaining agreement far easier than it might otherwise be. Since we know exactly what we want, and since what we want represents nothing more than what the individual is being paid to do, we start by describing the problem and asking for agreement.

Most individuals, most of the time, when approached by a manager calmly and professionally and asked to agree to do what they are getting paid to do, will agree. Will they live up to the agreement? We don't know, but we can never know during the meeting. All we can do during the meeting is gain the employee's agreement to change, secure in the knowledge that the odds are great that once a person agrees to solve a problem he will do so.

But let's say he doesn't agree. Let's say that George's response to our reasonable request that he agree to smoke only in designated areas is not agreement but objection.

"Oh, come on," George responds. "It's no big deal. I always ask the people around me if it's OK before I light up. If anybody ever says anything to me I put it right out. I waste a lot of time walking downstairs to the designated area and that's time taken away from my work. You used to smoke, too, you know. And you weren't as careful about lighting up around other people as I am. And look at the prez—he smokes anywhere he wants. Don't the rules apply to everybody? Just because he owns the joint does that mean he doesn't have to follow the rules he passes for us grunts? Why are you making such a big deal about such a little thing . . . don't you have anything more important to do?"

When managers are slammed with a salvo like that in response to an apparently simple request that a rule be followed, they usually respond in one of two unproductive ways. One, they may back off apologetically, since many of the things that George said are true (the president doesn't always model the behavior he asks of others; you used to be a smoker yourself; George is actually quite solicitous of others before he lights up). Or they may don their traditional armor of power and authority and respond to George: "I'm the boss; it's a rule; you'll do as you're told!"

"But wait a minute," managers typically react at this point. "Why bother with all this touchy-feely agreement stuff? The fact is, I *am* the boss. The fact is, it *is* a rule. If George doesn't like it, let him work somewhere else where the rules are different!"

To these managers I point out the obvious. Yes, you are the boss—you've got power. Yes, it is a rule—you've got authority. But do power and authority help you solve this problem and enhance your relationship with George? Do power and authority work?

Most managers will admit that having power and authority doesn't always give them the results they want, particularly when the results they seek involve more than mere compliance. The use of power can produce compliance, but commitment cannot be developed through authoritarian means.

Instead of power and authority, a more effective tactic is to seek agreement through considering the good business reasons why the problem must be solved and the consequences the employee will face if it is not.

Why is it important that a problem be solved? Why is it important that an individual agree to change once the existence of a problem has been brought to his attention? There must be good business reasons that caused the company to make the rule or create the expectation in the first place.

For George's problem of smoking in restricted areas, simply ask yourself, "What are the good business reasons why we don't allow smoking anywhere but in designated areas and outdoors? What difference does it make if someone smokes anyplace he chooses?"

A list of good business reasons usually flows forth without difficulty:

- The smell of smoke is offensive to many people.
- Breathing smoke is considered by some authorities to be a health hazard.
- Cigarette smoke, over time, interferes with the heating/venting/ air conditioning system, which increases costs.
- The presence of smoke in the workplace is distracting to others and causes them to complain or be distracted from what they are doing.
- Seeing George smoke in a restricted area without consequence is likely to suggest to others that the rules are there for appearances' sake only. Others are likely to start lighting up wherever they please.
- Many of the places in which smoking is restricted are off-limits for safety reasons as well as for the comfort and convenience of others. If George smokes in these areas he may be creating a safety hazard.

Two objectives are achieved by creating a list of good business reasons why it is important that the rule be obeyed and that the problem be solved. First, it increases the confidence of the manager in initiating the discussion. Once the manager has developed this list, he knows that the issue is not a trivial concern or merely a whim. There are substantive and important reasons why the rule or performance expectation exists.

Second, having a list of good business reasons why a problem must be solved increases the probability that the manager will be successful in gaining George's agreement to solve the problem and return to fully acceptable performance.

Most people will agree to solve a problem if it is brought to their attention in a mature, professional, and business-like way: "George, I have a problem. The company's smoking regulations provide that employees may smoke only in designated areas or outside the building, but I noticed this morning that you were smoking in the cafeteria. I need for you to agree that you'll restrict your smoking only to the appropriate areas from now on."

It would be difficult for George to refuse to agree if that statement was made to him in a serious and business-like way. But as we saw in the preceding example, George did fail to agree and instead responded that other people, including the president, also smoke in off-limits locations; that he always asked permission before smoking; and that walking from his work area to the smoking area wastes time. "Why are you making such a big deal about it?" asks George.

With your list of the problem's effects, you can now respond to George's objections confidently. "You're right, George. It does seem to be a minor problem. I can understand why you would think I'm making a mountain out of a molehill. But actually that's not the case. It really is important."

"Here's why," you continue. "When you smoke in an off-limits location it may bother other people, even though they may not complain directly to you. We want our employees to be free of any health risks and, whether you agree with them or not, there are a lot of doctors who say that secondhand smoke is dangerous. Your smoke gets into the ventilation system and increases the frequency of maintenance problems. And even though I have no control over what the president chooses to do, I can control how I work with people in my own unit. That's why I need for you to agree to smoke only where it's permitted."

Once again, it would be difficult for George to refuse. His boss has agreed with the fact that it is easy to believe that the smoking issue is a very minor problem. His boss has then explained, calmly and professionally, why smoking is restricted to certain areas. Finally, the boss closed the discussion by simply asking George to do no more than what he was getting paid to do—to follow the rules of the company.

Determining the Consequences

In rare cases people will refuse to agree to change their behavior even after they are told why their behavior creates a problem. In this case the manager must be prepared to explain the logical consequences of their choice not to do what they are getting paid to do.

In identifying the consequences that someone will face if she continues to perform unacceptably, we are simply advising the individual that the decisions she makes have consequences, as all decisions do. If she decides that in spite of knowing that what she is doing is a problem (missing deadlines, for example), and in spite of knowing why it's a problem (other people's work is delayed, her own projects get backed up, customers get poor service, managers in other units complain, etc.), she is still going to miss deadlines, there are logical consequences to that decision (like the denial of a merit increase, the refusal to assign the individual to more important and thus more satisfying projects, formal disciplinary transactions, closer supervision, etc.).

All decisions have consequences. The logical or natural consequences of an individual's decision to perform well, to exceed the organization's minimum standards, to offer assistance to others when one's own work is completed, to speak favorably of the organization with customers and colleagues and outsiders, to invest personal time in developmental activities, will be positive and rewarding.

On the other hand, if a person chooses to do only what she is told to do, to discuss only the negative aspects of life in the enterprise and the failures and shortcomings of her associates, to approach every assignment from the perspective of "What's in it for me?" and never go beyond minimum expectations, the consequences of those decisions will not be nearly as satisfying or rewarding.

Note that the approach just described does not involve the commission of any act for which disciplinary action would be appropriate. The person who chooses to remain just over the line of barely acceptable performance will not be subject to disciplinary action, since the steps of Discipline Without Punishment (or any other discipline system) are only appropriate when specific rules are violated or job performance becomes unacceptable. Maintaining a record of "barely acceptable" will not subject a person to the discipline system. But neither will it produce many of the organization rewards enjoyed by those whose commitment is much higher.

Every choice brings consequences. When an individual chooses to perform in a way that the organization finds unacceptable, and the individual chooses to continue that unacceptable behavior even after learning that it is unacceptable and the reasons why, the individual has the right to know what the consequences of that choice are. Certainly they will not be pleasant, but neither will they be threats. They will be straightforward descriptions of the logical, adverse consequences that can be expected when someone decides not to do what he is paid to do.

Generating the Consequences List

In generating the list of natural or logical consequences that are likely to result if the person chooses to continue inappropriate behavior, all managers immediately identify, "Further disciplinary action up to and including discharge."

When asked if there are any others, their initial attempts to expand the list usually involve simply restating the initial proposition:

"He'll be written up."
"She'll be subject to a Reminder 1."
"He will be suspended."
"She'll be fired."

While all of these are accurate, they are simply variations on the discipline theme. Are there not others?

Consider an employee who has developed an ongoing problem of doing personal work when she should be working. An informal conversation or two has failed to produce any significant change in her behavior. She still reads magazines and gossips in the break room and chats with her friends on the phone.

Her boss, in getting ready for a more serious Performance Improvement Discussion about the need to do only company business while she is on the clock, has no difficulty in identifying the difference between desired performance and actual performance. He also can easily enumerate the good business reasons why personal business must be attended to only on one's own time.

Describing the specifics of the problem itself and the effects of the problem will almost always be sufficient to bring about an agreement from the employee to straighten up and fly right. But if the manager's attempts to gain her agreement to do personal business on her own time are unsuccessful, the manager must be prepared to review the likely consequences that her decision will produce.

Certainly "further disciplinary action up to and including termination" will be on the list. But there are many other consequences that may turn out to be more powerful. For example:

Manager: "Connie, I'm disappointed that you still won't agree to do your personal business only on your own time and only work on company business while you're being paid."

Employee: "Yeah, but like I told you, I can't promise that I won't ever get any phone calls. If somebody decides to call me I can't stop them. And besides, when I'm finished with a big report, I like to take a couple minutes to catch my breath and switch gears for a minute. It's not like I'm spending all day reading novels. Gimme a break, huh?"

Manager: "Connie, I've told you that doing personal business is a problem and why it's a problem. I need for you to agree that you will do only what you're getting paid to do while you're getting paid to do it. If you decide to continue doing personal business, there are consequences to that decision."

Employee: "Like what?"

Manager: "If you decide to keep on doing personal things, that will cause me to decide to move into our discipline process."

Employee: "You'd write me up just for taking a phone call?"

Manager: "The decisions you make affect the decisions that I make. If you decide to continue your personal phone conversations then, yes, I will decide to continue forward with the discipline process. And there are other consequences, too."

Employee: "Like what?"

Manager: "Several things. If you decide not to correct this situation, that will cause me to decide to pay much closer attention to what you're doing. You can expect that I'll be moving you to a desk closer to my office so I can make sure that the problem has disappeared. I'm probably also going to decide not to allow you to participate on the annual event committee that you asked about last week."

Employee: "You'd keep me off that committee just because I don't spend every single minute with my nose to the grindstone?"

Manager: "If you decide not to do what you're getting paid to do, I have no way to justify letting you take time away from your basic job responsibilities. Yes, I would decide that."

Employee: "That's not fair . . ."

Manager: "What's not fair about that?"

Employee: "Well, I don't think you should keep me off the committee just because I was reading a magazine or something."

Manager: "Connie, the choices you make determine the choices I make. I have no desire to keep you off that committee. But the decision to be on the committee is yours, not mine. If you can agree to do what you're being paid to do and eliminate this problem of doing personal business, then it's easy for me to decide to release you for a special project. If you can't agree to that, then I have no way to justify letting you work on something that is actually less important than your basic job. So it's up to you."

Employee: "Well, I really want to do that committee thing."

Manager: "So what's your decision?"

Employee: "I'll do what you want."

Manager: "It's not 'what I want,' Connie. It's what the job requires. The basic job requirement is that you spend your work hours doing your work. I need for you to agree that you'll always do that. Can I have your agreement?"

Employee: "Sure."

Manager: "Good. I don't think we're ever going to have to talk about this again, are we?"

Employee: "No."

Manager: "I don't either. Let's get back to work."

In this case the manager was successful in gaining the employee's agreement to change. He got the agreement by reviewing the logical consequences if the employee failed to do what she was being paid to do.

But it is rare that the discussion will ever get to the point where the manager needs to review the list of consequences. Most people do their jobs well and never need any formal coaching about the need to make performance corrections. When problems do arise, most are quickly solved by an informal discussion without any advance preparation.

When a casual conversation fails to solve a problem and the manager moves to a more serious Performance Improvement Discussion, most of the time he will be successful simply by bringing the existence of the problem to the employee's attention, reviewing the good business reasons why the situation must be resolved, and asking the individual to agree to solve it. So only in rare cases when the employee consistently refuses to agree to change will the manager ever need to overtly describe the consequences of failure to perform properly. But even though the consequences list is rarely used, generating it increases the manager's self-confidence during the discussion.

A frequent misconception about identifying the logical consequences that someone will face if she chooses not to perform properly is that it is a list of the negative things that the manager is going to do if the employee continues her poor performance. But that's not quite right. Some of the consequences mentioned in the preceding dialogue certainly are actions that the manager will take: further disciplinary action, moving the employee's desk closer to the boss's office, refusing to let her participate on a special committee. But there may be other natural consequences of poor performance that are unrelated to anything that the manager might do. In the example, the manager might also have pointed out to Connie that a logical consequence if she continues doing personal business when she should be working is that she will lose her coworkers' respect and be less likely to be included in informal office social activities. Those negative consequences have nothing to with the manager. They are the logical outcomes of a decision not to perform as expected.

The manager's role is to help the individual make wise and rational decisions about job performance by pointing out that both performing well and performing poorly have consequences. Once the employee understands that decisions have consequences, she can make an informed decision to meet the standards of the organization, not because of threats or intimidation but because she understands fully the consequences of both meeting and failing to meet the standards of the organization.

Choosing a Course of Action

Having identified a problem in terms of both its category and the specific desired and actual performance, and having determined both the good business reasons why it must be solved and the consequences the employee will face if it's not, the manager can make a good decision about whether the discussion she will hold will be a nondisciplinary Performance Improvement Discussion or a formal disciplinary transaction. If a step of the Discipline Without Punishment procedure is appropriate, the analysis the manager has just completed, along with a review of any previous discussions, will indicate which of the formal levels of disciplinary action would be appropriate.

Whether the discussion is a Performance Improvement Discussion or a disciplinary transaction, the purpose of the meeting is the same: to get the employee to agree to change, correct the problem, and return to fully acceptable performance. In Chapter 5, I show you how to do that.

Conducting the Performance Improvement Discussion

Whether the discussion with the employee is a nondisciplinary Performance Improvement Discussion or a formal step of the Discipline Without Punishment system, the goal is the same: to get the employee to agree to solve the problem and return to fully acceptable performance. By securing the subordinate's agreement to correct the situation, the odds go up that an actual correction will result. If the correction does not follow and the problem continues, the next discussion will concentrate not only on the continuing problem but also on the subordinate's failure to live up to the agreement that she has made.

Before initiating the discussion, it is important to prepare fully, anticipate any difficulties that may arise, and create the conditions that will assure the highest probability of success.

In order to be fully prepared for the discussion, create a short written summary of the essential information that will be needed in the meeting. This information is simply the data that the manager collected in the previous step. The written summary should include brief statements of the following:

1. The Category the Problem Falls Into: Performance, Attendance, or Conduct. Noting the category at the top of the page will help get the conversation back on track if irrelevant issues take the discussion astray. This will also help the manager communicate that there is one specific area of performance that the manager is concerned with.

2. The Dates of Any Previous Conversations About This or Similar Problems. Having the actual dates available is invaluable, should the employee claim that this is the first time the issue has been raised.

What if the previous conversations were informal and no written record was made of them? The fact that no record was made does not negate the fact that they actually took place. If the employee says that he doesn't recall the conversation, acknowledge the fact that sometimes people do forget things and that's why you went to the trouble of jotting down some notes about the discussion. Then suggest that the subordinate make a note of the fact that the two of you are talking now, because the situation has now become more serious.

What if you can't recall the specific date? Again, just because you can't come up with the precise date that the conversation occurred doesn't discount the fact that it did in fact happen. Simply estimate the date as accurately as possible: "We talked about this around three weeks ago, Walt, and at that time. . . ."

3. Specific Statements of Desired Performance and Actual Performance. This is the most important part of the written summary. Here the manager writes, in simple, clear, and unarguable terms, exactly what the performance expectation is and precisely how the employee is failing to meet that expectation.

In the attendance category both the expectation and the actual performance will be quite easy to specify. The *desired* performance is for the employee to arrive at work on time every day; the *actual* performance is that on May 5, 11, 22, and 26, Sally Edwards reported for work more than twenty minutes late.

Similarly, when the problem is in the conduct area, the difference between actual and desired is usually very clear: The *desired* performance is that supervisors wait until the Personnel Change Notice form is returned by the compensation department before advising an employee that he has been granted a salary increase; the *actual* performance is that Marilyn Longer told George Schmidt that he would be getting a raise before the paperwork was processed.

In the performance area the difference between what we want and what we get may be murky. It may be difficult to pinpoint one specific behavior, or even a collection of specific shortcomings, that creates the need for a formal discussion. In these cases, the manager should continually ask herself: "For example . . . ?" as she attempts to move her generalizations and judgments about the individual into accurate and defensible illustrations of performance deficiencies.

4. A Summary of the Good Business Reasons the Problem Needs to Be Solved. Compiling a list of the effects of the problem helps the employee understand why what he is doing is a problem. It also helps produce the employee's agreement to solve that problem.

To generate a complete list, assume that the individual has said, "I don't really think that what I am doing is a problem. What difference does it make?" How would you respond?

Most managers find it fairly easy to generate a list of a half dozen good business reasons why a problem must be solved, particularly when they consider the impact of the situation on fellow employees, customers (both internal and external), the culture of the organization, the perceptions of others, and the effects on the manager himself.

5. A List of Likely Consequences if the Individual Chooses Not to Change and Correct the Situation. One consequence that will always appear on the list will be, "Further disciplinary action up to and including discharge."

While managers usually view the potential for disciplinary action as a serious consequence for misbehavior, employees frequently discount both the likelihood and severity of the threat. Marginal employees may have heard managers thunder, "I'm gonna write you up!" or "I'll fire you if you ever do that again!" so many times that they consider this just one more manipulative game managers play to enforce order and get more work out of the troops. Constantly threatened with write-ups and sackings, they become deaf to the warning of further disciplinary action.

Unable to see past the threat of "further disciplinary action," managers often overlook responses that may have far more persuasive power with difficult employees. If a person refuses to correct a deficiency once it has been brought to his attention, the likely outcomes— being denied salary increases and promotional opportunities, or being subjected to closer supervision and assigned to less desirable tasks— may be far more persuasive in convincing the employee of the need to change.

With these notes prepared, the manager is now fully ready to begin the discussion with a high probability that both an improvement in performance and an enhanced relationship will result.

The Five Classic Questions

A half-century ago, Arbitrator Carroll Daugherty, in rendering his decision in the *Grief Bros. Cooperage* arbitration case, provided a series of tests to determine "whether employer had just and proper cause for disciplining an employee."[1] As Daugherty explained it, "a *no* answer to any one or more of the following questions normally signifies that just and proper cause did not exist." These tests can be boiled down to five questions that every manager should ask himself before proceeding with a disciplinary discussion.

The five questions are these:

1. Did the employee clearly understand the rule or policy that was violated?
2. Did the employee know in advance that such conduct would be subject to disciplinary action?
3. Was the rule violated reasonably related to the safe, efficient, and orderly operation of the business?
4. Is there substantial evidence that the employee actually did violate the rule?
5. Is the action planned reasonably related to the seriousness of the offense, the employee's record with the organization, and to ac-

tion taken with other employees who have committed a similar offense?[2]

Reviewing these questions and getting affirmative answers to each one assures you that you are on solid ground in taking the action you have planned. Even more important, if any disciplinary action or discharge is ever challenged, the organization's ability to demonstrate that all managers consider Daugherty's tests before taking action greatly increases the defensibility of whatever action was taken.

Creating the Setting

Too often the decisions about when the meeting for the Performance Improvement Discussion will be held, who will be present, the location of the meeting, where participants will sit, the time allotted to it, and other critical matters are made by default. The more that these issues are resolved consciously, the greater the likelihood of overall success.

Where Should the Meeting Be Held?

While the logical place is in the manager's office, there are alternatives to consider. If privacy is a concern, consider using a conference room. If the matter is not yet serious enough to invoke one of the formal Discipline Without Punishment steps, a session at an isolated table in the cafeteria might be effective. If the matter is a very serious disciplinary transaction, the manager may ask his or her boss if the meeting can be scheduled in the boss's office, with the senior manager present as a witness to increase the perceived seriousness of the issue.

When Should the Meeting Be Held?

The session should follow the discovery of the problem as closely as possible, but sufficient time must be allowed for the manager to investigate the facts and prepare for the meeting.

Too often, managers begin the discussion with an employee about a problem immediately upon uncovering a serious lapse in acceptable performance. By rushing pell-mell into a discussion, the manager loses effectiveness in two ways. First, since he took no time to prepare, he has not thought through the issues of desired and actual performance, the effects and the logical consequences, and thus will be less capable of avoiding distractions and maintaining a professional approach. Worse, since the manager took no time to prepare, the employee may believe that this is merely a spur-of-the-moment reaction on the manager's part and not a matter of serious concern.

Another scheduling issue involves getting all the necessary approvals before beginning the discussion. In almost every organization a supervisor must get higher management approval before proceeding with one of the more serious steps of the Discipline Without Punishment procedure. No organization I have ever worked with allows a manager to place an employee on Decision Making Leave or terminate the individual without at least a review by the Human Resources function and a member of the senior management team. These reviews frequently take time, and as the time between the commission of the act and the discussion of the issue expands, the impact of the discussion on the employee may decrease.

Effective implementation of the complete Discipline Without Punishment procedure always simplifies the approval process, but time obstacles created by out-of-town trips, vacations of key approvers, and other schedule dilemmas may still interfere with discussing the matter with all deliberate speed. When time delays occur, it may be wise to say to the employee, "This situation is one that concerns me a great deal and we will need to talk about it seriously. I will get back to you as soon as I can and set a time for a meeting to discuss it. In the meantime, it is important that you immediately follow all job procedures."

Of course, in some situations the employee's presence on the premises cannot be tolerated during the investigation period. Later, in discussing the procedures for a "Crisis Suspension" in Chapter 10, we explore in detail how to handle these difficult and complex situations.

What Are the Room Arrangements?

Room arrangements rarely make much difference in achieving the goal of gaining the employee's agreement. The most important decision the supervisor needs to make is whether she wishes to increase her perceived power or increase the informal nature of the meeting.

If the problem is essentially minor and the supervisor does not want to come across as overbearing, moving out from behind the desk and sitting at a conference table or some other more egalitarian setting may have the desired effect. On the other hand, it may well be appropriate for the supervisor to deliberately increase her perceived power. In this case, such minor items as putting on her suit coat, sitting behind the desk, maintaining a firm and upright posture, and removing all paper from the desk except for the notes she had made for the conversation communicate a grave atmosphere that may produce serious reflection.

(In a recent seminar, a manager admitted that he had secretly placed both a telephone directory and a dictionary on his chair before meeting with a particularly recalcitrant troublemaker. Being able to look down on the individual greatly increased his perceived power in the situation.)

Who Should Participate?

The two principal players are the employee and the immediate supervisor. Everyone else is secondary.

If the employee is represented by a union, the shop steward or other union representative should be present during the discussion. If the discussion is intended to be a formal disciplinary transaction, it should not begin without the presence of the appropriate union representative. Even if the discussion is planned to be a nondisciplinary Performance Improvement Discussion, it is often wise to ask the employee if he wants a union representative to be present and to advise the union representative about the problem and the discussion the manager had about it.

While the presence of a union representative often may appear to make it more difficult to conduct a productive discussion, the representative's presence may reinforce the idea with the employee that this is indeed serious business. Even if the shop steward is combative and confrontational during the meeting, it may well be that after the session has ended, as the employee and the steward are walking back to the workplace, the steward may throw a friendly arm around the employee's shoulder and say, "Look, pal. I put on a show in there for you. But you need to know that you're in trouble. If you keep this up there's not much that the union will be able to do for you."

Should other members of management be present? The two who most often attend these discussions are the supervisor's immediate boss and a representative from the HR department. Think small. Usually, the more people present, the less effective the discussion. The employee may feel overpowered and ganged up on; in this case he is likely to agree to anything just to get out of the situation, with no real intention of following through on any glib commitment to change.

Worse, the opposite situation may happen. The employee may be able to play one person off another, listening to one person and redirecting questions to someone else, so that nothing of substance gets accomplished.

There may be reasons to have witnesses present during the conversation, but their role should be just that: a witness, not a significant participant. The primary reasons for having a witness present are:

- To increase the perceived level of seriousness by the employee. This is particularly beneficial at the later stages of disciplinary action.

- To confirm the supervisor's recollection of exactly what happened during the meeting if required at a later date, particularly if there is any concern that an employee may be untruthful about what was said in the meeting.

- In cases where the supervisor is unskilled in conducting disciplinary transactions, to allow a "coach" for the supervisor to be present if needed. In this case, the supervisor and the other individual should discuss in advance the conditions under which the "coach" would become an active participant in the transaction.

- If there is any concern that the employee may become confrontational or violent, a third person in the room may serve as a calming influence.
- If there is any concern that the employee may accuse the supervisor of sexual harassment of other inappropriate behavior during the discussion, having a witness present diminishes this possibility. This consideration is particularly important when a male supervisor is having a performance discussion with a female subordinate.
- In cases where the issue to be discussed is either extremely complicated technically or there are specific legal aspects to the situation, to make sure that the technical or legal aspects are properly addressed.

How Long Should the Meeting Take?

The time devoted to the meeting will vary depending on the subject to be discussed and the players involved. The most common problem is that meetings like this take too much time, rather than not enough. It is usually more effective to have more short and well-planned meetings than a few long meetings that ramble and meander.

The time of the meeting should be proportionate to the goals to be accomplished. In every meeting the primary goal is to gain the employee's agreement to solve the problem. The manager gains the employee's agreement by reviewing exactly what the problem is and by then asking for the employee's agreement to correct the situation. Even if the manager has to go beyond describing the problem itself and discuss the adverse effects and the logical consequences, probably not more than five minutes or so will be necessary.

Once agreement has been gained, more time may be spent on reviewing the possible actions the employee might take to solve the problem. It may be appropriate to engage in some mutual goal setting or for the manager and the employee to develop a joint plan of action. There may be great value in requiring the employee to construct a PIP (Performance Improvement Plan) that they will review in a subsequent meeting. There may be still other issues that arise during the course of the discussion that are worth talking about while the manager and subordinate are together, once the basic agreement has been achieved.

If the transaction is a formal disciplinary discussion, a few minutes will be taken to explain to the employee that this is a formal level of the Discipline Without Punishment procedure. The manager needs to review the organization's procedures and explain how the incident will be documented.

With all this, the total time devoted to the discussion, from the time the employee enters the office until the participants shake hands and get back to work, rarely needs to extend more than twenty minutes.

With all preliminary procedures and requirements settled, the manager can begin the actual Performance Improvement Discussion or disciplinary transaction.

Opening the Discussion

Perhaps the most difficult ten seconds in a manager's life occur at the moment when a subordinate shows up at his door for a scheduled Performance Improvement Discussion or disciplinary discussion, sticks his head in and says, "You wanted to see me, Boss?"

The manager knows that if he is able to get the meeting off to a good start, the chances of overall success will be great. But if the meeting gets off to a bad start, if the discussion sputters and becomes awkward, he may spend the whole time simply trying to get things back to normal. How do you get things off to a good start?

The conventional advice is accurate: Put the employee at ease. But the conventional suggestion about how to put the individual at ease—talk about matters other than the subject at hand—invariably serves to worsen the situation. Managers often are given wrongheaded advice, such as warm up to the subject by talking about how things are going at home, or spend a minute on her hobbies or interests. Having swallowed a dose of this psychological snake oil, the manager starts the conversation off with a chipper discussion of how the local ball team is doing. Worse, the manager may start by asking, "How are things going?" and then, when the employee responds that things are terrific and that no problems of any kind exist, will be in the awkward position of having to disabuse the individual of his notion that all is well.

Stop the palaver. When the manager asks the employee to meet with him for a discussion, the employee knows that the manager has a specific concern, and that concern has little to do with the fortunes of the local ball club or how the garden is coming along. How, then can the manager put the employee at ease?

By getting right to the point.

"Joe," the manager begins, "I've got a problem and I need your help." With those ten words, the manager has accomplished four worthwhile ends. First, simply by using the employee's name he has begun the discussion on a personal basis. One of the most effective ways of enhancing an individual's self-esteem is the remarkably simple technique of using the employee's name. It is virtually impossible to overdo it.

Second, the manager has indeed gotten right to the point. In hardly a second he has let the employee know that the subject of the meeting is a problem that concerns the manager—not the doings of the ball team, or life at home with the wife and the kids, or things in general around the office.

Third, by using an "I-message," the manager has prevented the immediate defensiveness that arises when the discussion begins with a heavy "you" emphasis. At this point it is the manager who has a concern; it is the manager who is raising the issue; it is the manager who feels the need for action. At the end of the meeting, the employee may well have a problem. At the start of the meeting, however, defensiveness can be reduced by using an "I-statement" rather than opening with a variation on the accusatory, "You're causing some difficulties that I need to talk to you about . . ." or "You're doing something that you need to stop . . ." or "You've got a problem!"

Finally, in his opening words the manager has enlisted the employee's help. There seems to be magic contained in the phrase, "I've got a problem and I need your help." The psychologists may explain it in terms of our needs to be fulfilled or self-actualized, our need for achievement or desire to be of service. Whatever the reason, the phrase has the uncommon ability to make people immediately react in a way that puts them at your service.

A Good Opening Statement

To get the meeting off on a good start, open with either those exact words or a close variant:

> "Sally, there's something that's concerning me and I need to talk to you about it."

> "Ed, I'm dealing with a situation that's troubling me. I need your help in getting it resolved."

> "Chris, there's something that's bothering me and I need to see if I can get your help in getting it taken care of."

The use of the magic phrase, "I've got a problem and I need your help," will command the individual's attention. Then immediately move to a full description of the concern you just introduced. Explain the problem in terms of actual and desired behavior:

> "At the start of the year, Lucille, you and I agreed that you would visit every site location at least twice during the year. We're now into September and your reports indicate that you've been to less than half the sites, and some of those visits were only for an hour or so."

> "Here's the issue, Tony. Right or wrong, the company expects that nobody will put any software on their computer without requisitioning it through central supply and paying for it. Louise told me that she was concerned about your borrowing her disks for the Micro-Cad program and installing it on your machine."

> "You know that the roller cover is put on the machine as a safety guard, Dan. A week ago I pointed out that you were running the machine with the cover raised. Then this morning I again saw you running the machine without the cover in place."

> "Charlie, remember that training program we all went through a month or so ago called Building Team Effectiveness? My goal for putting all of us through that was to get us to start acting more like a team and less like a bunch of individual contributors. I tried to say that during the program and when we did the debriefing afterwards. But I haven't seen you act in the ways we talked about during the session. Here's what I mean . . . in Charlene's review meeting yesterday afternoon you were late getting in and then spent most of the time going through the papers you brought with you. When Jack asked for help in doing the final clearcheck on the turbine outflow, you were the only one who didn't contribute. As I recall, what you said was, 'Hey, pal, my bucket's full . . .' And then this morning you complained that you would need to change your flight plans if we held the Osbourne final run-through at a time that worked out perfectly for everyone but you. I noticed a couple other things, but those are the main ones that concern me."

In each case, the manager clearly communicated exactly what the desired behavior was and exactly how the employee was failing to meet the expectation.

Some of the situations are easy identify and to explain to the employee. Lucille either visited all of the sites or she didn't; Dan either was working with the safety guard on or he was not. Both what we want and what we get are clear.

The other situations are not so clear cut. The manager did not accuse Tony of being a software pirate. Instead he stuck to what he knew for sure: that Louise had expressed a concern about his borrowing her disks and installing the program on his machine.

The last situation is the most difficult: Charlie's failure to act as a team player. In this case there is not a specific deviation from a clearly defined standard. Instead, Charlie's boss has noticed a collection of behaviors that, while individually minor and perhaps insignificant, taken together support his contention that Charlie is not acting as part of a team. He described three very specific incidents that supported his conclusion that the broader goal of having everyone support each other as a team was not being met.

Note that in none of these statements made to begin the discussion does the manager accuse the employee or hypothesize about what might be causing the problem. In a straightforward, businesslike way, the manager simply makes three statements:

"Here's what I want."
"Here's what I get."
"There is a difference."

Letting the Employee Speak

Having opened the discussion with the useful phrase, "I have a problem and I need your help," and having stated clearly the specific desired and actual performance, the manager now turns the conversational ball over to the employee by saying, "Tell me about it."

Too often, managers lose effectiveness in their coaching or disciplinary discussions because they talk too much. They talk too much because they are nervous. The situation is difficult and unfamiliar; there is a lot at stake; they don't know exactly what to say or what the employee's reaction will be; they feel awkward and ill-prepared. So the way they resolve their awkward and uncomfortable feelings is by talking. But the more they talk, the less effective they become.

Ask any manager for his recommendation about who should do the most talking in a coaching session and he will instantly tell you: the employee. But tune in to a typical conversation and you'll discover that it's the manager who's talking far more than 50 percent of the time.

The reason that managers talk so much in the opening of the transaction is that they don't know how to hand off the conversational ball to the employee gracefully. All that it takes, however, is the simple phrase, "Tell me about it," or some minor variant on the theme.

The model for opening the conversation is straightforward and direct: "I've got a problem and I need your help. Here's what it is. . . . Tell me about it." And then the manager shuts up and lets the employee speak.

The use of the exact phrase, "Tell me about it," is not critical. Many other transition statements will work equally well:

"What can you tell me about this?"
"Is there something I should know?"
"Is my understanding accurate?"

In each case, the phrase serves to turn the responsibility for the conversation over to the employee without raising the individual's defensiveness. The goal is problem solving, not accusation. Asking the employee, "What have you got to say for yourself?" will probably not achieve this end.

Each of the preceding examples of opening transactions involved at most ten to twenty seconds—a far shorter period than most managers spend in getting the discussion under way. But one of the reasons why this approach is so effective is that it is so short: The manager says nothing that will give the employee an opportunity to rebut the manager's statement unless the manager is simply flat dead wrong. And in those unusual cases where the manager has initiated a discussion based on bad data, the effect of using this opening will reduce the awkwardness since there have been no accusations or threats of disciplinary action made.

Having turned the discussion over to the employee, the manager's job is now to listen to what the employee has to say.

But ask a manager, "What are you listening for?" and he will experience great confusion. Instead of telling you exactly what he is listening for, he will explain why listening is a good thing. It communicates an interest in what the employee has to say, he responds. It helps build the relationship; it may provide information on the cause of the problem or the possible solutions that might be employed to correct it.

Listening carefully certainly indicates that you really are interested in what the other person has to say. By listening you send a message that the other person—his feelings and perceptions—are really important to you. You get a better understanding of someone else and how that person looks at things.

The Key Aim of Listening

While all of the things just mentioned are true, there is one specific objective that we have when we listen to the employee in the opening of a Performance Improvement Discussion or disciplinary transaction: *We listen specifically to confirm that the action we have planned is appropriate.*

At this point in the transaction you have identified the problem in terms of desired and actual behavior. You have determined the effects of the problem and the logical consequences that the employee can expect if she chooses not to correct the situation. Based on that, you have also determined what you feel is the appropriate action to take.

But up to this point, you haven't talked to the person. And while it doesn't happen very often, it is possible that there may be some additional information that you are unaware of that could cause you to change your mind about what the best course of action should be.

For example, let's say that you notice one morning that one of your employees is not at his desk. Since you have had two previous discussions about his tardiness problem, you decide to conduct a formal Reminder 1 discussion with him as soon as he comes in.

You begin the conversation by saying, "Bill, I have a problem. We've talked twice before about the importance of being at work on time every day and once again you're late. Is there anything that I need to be aware of?"

But instead of offering the anticipated lame excuse, Bill says, "Yeah, there sure is! Yes, I was late getting in, but the reason I was late was that just as I was coming in, the shop superintendent saw me and told me that there had been an accident near the tooling shed and to go to the back gate and watch for the ambulance and send it to the shed when they arrived!" In this case, any form of formal disciplinary action would probably be inappropriate. But had the manager opened the discussion by saying, "Bill, I called you in here to give you a Reminder 1 for coming in late this morning," he would find it difficult to proceed once Bill reveals the reason for his tardiness. Assuming that Bill is telling the truth, the manager is now in the awkward position of either having to retract something he has already announced or to proceed with something he no longer feels is appropriate.

That's why you have one specific purpose in listening to the employee: to confirm that there is no other information that could cause you to change your decision about the appropriate action to take. For this reason it is best to wait until the end of the conversation to announce to the employee that the discussion is a formal disciplinary transaction, unless by union contract the supervisor is required to tell the employee that the discussion is disciplinary before he can begin.

Gaining the Employee's Agreement

Once you have listened to the employee's response and confirmed that there is no reason not to proceed with the action you have planned, discuss the situation with the objective of gaining the person's agreement to change.

Most of the time you'll be able to get the employee's agreement to solve a problem simply by asking for it. Review your statements of actual and desired performance and then ask the employee to agree to do the job as it should be done:

Manager: "Janet, I've got a problem and I need your help."

Employee: "A problem?"

Manager: "Yeah. Remember two weeks ago when Morley called about the Harrison estimate? You said you'd get on it right away but apparently nothing's happened. He called me this morning and he was livid. What's the story?"

Employee: "Well, to tell you the truth I got behind on it and I didn't get it out. There's been so much going on that a couple of things are bound to fall through the cracks. I'll take care of it right away."

Manager: "I know we're busy, but this is now the third time we've had to talk about getting project work done as scheduled. I mentioned it to you last month and then a few weeks ago we talked specifically about deadlines when the Lanaham deadline was missed. I'm concerned about the Harrison estimate, but my real concern is that you aren't getting your jobs done on time."

Employee: "Well, I've just been busy . . . it's been crazy around here for a while."

Manager: "I know that. I also know that the work we accept has to be produced when it's due. I need for you to agree that in the future every project you've got will be finished on the agreed date."

Employee: "Well, I do try, but sometimes things get in the way."

Manager: "I know they do. If a problem comes up, I need for you to come and talk to me as soon as you see the deadline is in trouble. But I do need your agreement that you'll meet those deadlines every time."

Employee: "Well I guess I can do that . . ."

Manager: "What do you mean?"

Employee: "I mean that I will meet all of the deadlines from now on."

Manager: "That's great, Janet. Can we consider this case closed?"

Employee: "Sure. Case closed."

Manager: "Thanks."

In this case the manager was clear about the gap between actual and desired performance and clearly asked for the employee's agreement to solve the problem: "I need for you to agree that in the future every project you've got will be out on the agreed date." When the employee made an initial move in the direction of providing the agreement, the manager confirmed that the agreement was real. To her statement of, "I guess I can do that . . ." the manager responded, "What do you mean?" The result was a clear statement of her agreement to meet the expectation: "I mean that I will meet all of the deadlines from now on."

Most people will agree to solve the problems they create once those problems have been brought to their attention in a calm, professional, business-like way. Occasionally the manager may need to explain the adverse effects caused by the problem in order to provoke the agreement:

Manager: "Thanks for coming in, Sal. There's an issue that's concerning me that I need to get your help in resolving."

Employee: "Sure, what's the trouble?"

Manager: "Calls and contacts."

Employee: "Calls and contacts? We just talked about that a week or so ago and now you want to talk about it again?"

Manager: "That's right, Sal. When we talked last time I went over exactly what expectations we have for you and everybody else in telephone sales. It's sixteen calls an hour, sixteen contacts a day. You're still a long way away . . . what's the problem?"

Employee: "Sixteen/sixteen's is an awful lot. Besides, I make better contacts than anybody else. Almost every one of the contacts I make ends up being a buyer. Nobody else gets the quality of contacts that I do. It's quality that's important, not quantity, isn't it?"

Manager: "Quality is important, Sal, and I've got no problems with the quality of contacts you make."

Employee: "Damn right."

Manager: "But that's not the issue. I need for you to agree that you will meet the basic expectation of making a minimum of sixteen calls an hour, and out of those make direct contact with sixteen qualified prospects every day."

Employee: "I can't promise that. I can't control who answers the phones or the kinds of leads I get."

Manager: "Do you know why it's important, Sal?"

Employee: "Because you say so."

Manager: "Not because I say so. Because it actually does make a difference. That standard has been in place for almost two years and it's a reasonable one. If we don't have a target then we don't know how we're doing. If you don't make your calls, other people figure it's not important. They start sliding too."

Employee: "Well talk to them, then."

Manager: "I do. I talk to everyone who doesn't make the sixteen/sixteen standard. That's why we're talking now, Sal. I know that you can do it—I just need you to agree that you will."

Employee: "And if I don't?"

Manager: "You know the answer to that. We'll talk again, but this time it will be a formal disciplinary transaction. I'll also require that you report your results to me on an hour-by-hour basis."

Employee: "Like we were back in fourth grade, huh?"

Manager: "Sal, come on. I don't want to ask you for hourly reports any more than you want to be forced to provide them. What I do want is for you to agree to solve this problem and get back to doing the job right. Can I have your agreement?"

Employee: "Yeah, sure."

Manager: "Sal, what are you actually agreeing to do?"

Employee: "I'm agreeing to do what you're telling me I gotta do."

Manager: "And what is that?"

Employee: "To make sixteen calls an hour and generate sixteen good contacts a day."

Manager: "Will you do it?"

Employee: "Yeah, I'll do it."

Manager: "Sal, are we ever going to have to talk about this again?"

Employee: "No. I'll get it done."

Manager: "Do we have a deal?"

Employee: "Sure."

In this case the manager had to discuss both the adverse effects of the problem and the logical consequences if the employee failed to meet the expectations. But focusing on the specific issue allowed the manager to gain the agreement and close the conversation on a productive note.

Whatever the subject to be discussed, and regardless of whether the transaction is a nondisciplinary Performance Improvement Discussion, a Reminder 1, or a Reminder 2, the procedure is the same:

1. Open the conversation by getting directly to the point: I have a problem; here's what it is; tell me about it.
2. Listen to what the employee has to say to make sure that the action you are planning to take is appropriate.
3. Ask the employee for agreement. If you gain agreement, wrap the discussion up. If you fail to gain agreement, discuss the adverse effects of the problem and, if necessary, the logical consequences the employee will face if he chooses not to correct the situation.
4. End the discussion by communicating a positive expectation of change.

What if the Problem Continues?

The individual has agreed to solve a problem, but the problem arises again. What next?

Obviously, another conversation with the individual is held. This time, two additional steps are taken:

1. The manager reviews the employee's failure to live up to the previous agreement.
2. The manager and the employee explore the specific action the employee will take to assure a permanent correction of the situation.

In the initial conversation, the manager and the employee may have discussed various things that the individual might do to make sure that the problem is be corrected. In many cases the steps that the person must take are obvious. Certainly for problems in the conduct category, the solution is plain: Follow the rule. For an employee with a problem of smoking in a restricted area, no complicated plan of action is required to eliminate it. She simply must not smoke where it's not permitted.

Problems in the performance and attendance categories may take more planning and action on the employee's part to solve:

Manager: "Michael, when we talked last time you agreed that we would never have to talk about your coming to work late again. But the problem continues. What's going on?"

Employee: "Well, Becky, when we talked before I didn't know that my wife was going to be switched to the 3-to-11 shift at the hospital. And I certainly didn't know that the transmission and the brakes on my car would both give out at the same time. These things happen. Give me a break."

Manager: "These things do happen, Michael, and if you had brought them to my attention I'm sure we could have worked something out. But when you decide not to let me know about what's going on and choose to deal with your problems by coming into work late, those decisions on your part affect the decisions that I make."

Employee: "Wait a minute! I didn't *decide* not to tell you, I just forgot. I didn't *choose* to come to work late. It just happened, that's all."

Manager: "Michael, those things really are decisions and choices. You are responsible for arranging your affairs so that you can do what we pay you to do. At a minimum, that means showing up. When you decide not to do that, whether it's a conscious decision or not, I have to deal with the decisions and choices you make."

Employee: "I want to be here every day. I really do. I just ran into shot of bad luck, that's all."

Manager: "This is serious, Michael. I need for you to agree that you will be here on time every day."

Employee: "I'll try . . ."

Manager: "I'm glad you'll try, Michael, but what I need is a real commitment."

Employee: "Ok, I'll be here every day."

Manager: "On time?"

Employee: "On time."

Manager: "How will you do that?"

Employee: "Huh?"

Manager: "You agreed to be here every day on time in our last conversation, Michael, but you didn't live up to it. What are you going to do different this time so you can honor that commitment?"

Employee: "Well, like I said, I'll try harder."

Manager: "Come on, Michael. What are you really going to do?"

Employee: "I'm taking the car in to the shop tomorrow and I can arrange for a ride with Roy in case it's not ready. With Judy's 3-to-11 shift I'll need to leave here right on time to pick up the kids at the day care, but that shouldn't be a problem. And I can make a backup arrangement with Roy in case I run into car problems again."

Manager: "Will you do that?"

Employee: "Yeah."

Manager: "Do we have an agreement?"

Employee: "Yeah, we do."

Revisiting the Agreement

It may happen that in spite of making an original agreement to correct a problem, an individual continues the inappropriate behavior even after a subsequent conversation in which the agreement was reviewed and various alternative solutions that would assure that the person could live up to his agreement were discussed. In this case, the manager needs to be blunt about the consequences of the person's choice not to honor an agreement that he has made. At this point the problem is no longer merely a continuation of the original incident. The real problem is the employee's failure to live up to his agreement:

> *Manager*: "Sal, two weeks ago we talked about calls and contacts. At that time you agreed that you would make sixteen calls an hour and sixteen contacts a day. I just got the weekly summary from last week. You averaged thirteen calls and nine contacts."
>
> *Employee*: "Yeah, but it was a tough week, and some of those calls took a real long time. I'll do better next week."
>
> *Manager*: "Doing better isn't the issue any more, Sal."
>
> *Employee*: "You mean thirteen calls and nine contacts is OK?"
>
> *Manager*: "No. It's unacceptable and you know that it's unacceptable. But that's not what we're here to talk about."
>
> *Employee*: "It's not?"
>
> *Manager*: "No. What I need to talk to you about is your agreement. You agreed that you would make sixteen calls an hour and sixteen contacts a day and you decided not to live up to it."
>
> *Employee*: "Yeah, but I meant to."
>
> *Manager*: "Whatever your intentions were, Sal, the fact is still the same: You made an agreement with your boss, and you decided not to honor it."
>
> *Employee*: "Well, gee, I didn't look at it that way."
>
> *Manager*: "Is there something wrong with looking at it that way?"
>
> *Employee*: "No, not exactly, but it sounds real serious when you put it like that."
>
> *Manager*: "It is serious, and that is exactly the right way to put it. Tell me something, Sal. If you decide not to live up to the agreements that you make with your customers, what do you think will happen?"

Employee: "They'll stop doing business with me."

Manager: "That's right. And what will happen if you decide not to live up to the agreements you make with your boss?"

Employee: "You'll fire me?"

Manager: "Yes, Sal, I will. If you choose not to honor your agreements, what basis do we have for an employment relationship?"

Employee: "Well, if you put it like that, I guess we don't have any basis."

Manager: "That's right. That's why it's important, when you make an agreement, that you live up to it. Now are you able to agree to make the sixteen calls and sixteen contacts?"

Employee: "I guess I really don't have any choice."

Manager: "Not if you want to work here you don't. You know exactly what the job requires, Sal—the question is, do you still want it?"

Employee: "Yeah. Of course I want my job."

Manager: "Then I need for you to agree that you'll do what's required."

Employee: "Well, sure. Now that you put it that way, of course I agree."

Manager: "That's great, Sal. Now let's talk about what you need to do to make sure that you can actually live up to that agreement . . ."

A Matter of Choice

In the previous two examples, the manager concentrated on talking to the employee in terms of "decisions" and "choices." As the manager in the first example said, "But when you *decide* not to let me know about what's going on and *choose* to deal with your problems by coming into work late, those decisions on your part affect the decisions that I make." In the second example the manager said, "You agreed that you would make sixteen calls an hour and sixteen contacts a day and you *decided* not to live up to it."

One of the fundamental principles of Discipline Without Punishment is the recognition that performing well or poorly, coming to work on time or late, following or breaking the rules, and living up to or disregarding one's agreements are matters of choice. The communication process used in all Discipline Without Punishment transactions reinforces this basic idea that people are responsible for their behavior and performance. The concept of personal responsibility for one's own actions is the essence of Discipline Without Punishment.

Locus of Control

Many people who encounter performance problems in organizations and fail to live up to their agreements believe that they have little control over what happens to them and that they are, for the most part, pawns of fate. The psychological term for this phenomenon is *locus of control.* Locus of control refers to the extent to which individuals believe that they can exert control over the events that affect them. Some people (*Internalizers*) see themselves as masters of their own fate, captains of their own souls. They believe that they are autonomous and take personal responsibility for what happens to them— good or bad. They believe that the events of their lives, for the most part, are a function of their actions and decisions. Their "locus of control" is internal.

Other people (*Externalizers*) believe that they ultimately bear little personal responsibility for what happens to them or for their actions and decisions. Those with an external locus of control believe that events in their lives are primarily determined by factors outside their control—by chance, by fate, by other people. Externalizers will argue that making a lot of money is simply a matter of getting the right breaks; Internalizers believe that raises are earned by hard work. Externalizers are likely to say that it's just about impossible to figure some people out; Internalizers will argue that getting along with people is a skill which must be practiced. Internalizers believe that their choices regarding diet and exercise will have a direct effect on their health; Externalizers point to runners who die young and smokers who live to be ninety and say, "You never can tell." Internalizers believe that they can change the world around them; Externalizers believe that it is pointless to try.

On tests of "locus of control," most managers achieve high *Internalizer* scores. They tend to be more achievement oriented and are comfortable with the idea that we are responsible for the choices we make and for the things that happen to us. A person with a low *Internalizer* score would probably be neither happy nor successful as a manager, since we expect managers to exert influence over the world and the people around them.

With their Internalizer view of the world, managers can be frustrated when confronted with an individual with an external locus of control. Not only will the Externalizer subordinate be likely to write off any failure to meet expectations as simply a matter of "that's the way the ball bounces," the Externalizer will also be less likely to accept praise or compliments on a job well done—"Thanks, but it wasn't really me," he is likely to respond. "I just got lucky this time around. That's how it goes sometimes."

The difficulty with managing the Externalizer is the individual's inability or reluctance to connect his own choices of behavior with the consequences that those choices produce. If life truly is a matter of luck, chance, and fate, then it is as misguided to reward people with a perfect attendance record as it is to punish those whose absenteeism is intolerable. *Que sera, sera.*

Most managers reject the Externalizer's argument that chance plays the dominant role in determining what happens to us. The Internalizer manager points out that among the common characteristics of those people who had perfect attendance records were that they maintained a regular exercise program; they maintained their weight and ate a healthy diet; they took good care of their cars and had a backup plan if their cars ever developed problems; they got up in the morning early enough that they could leave for work with a sufficient margin of time that an unforeseen traffic jam didn't make them late; and so on.

It is about as difficult to convince a person with an external locus of control to take personal responsibility for his behavior as it would be to explain to a highly successful manager that her success is simply a function of good luck . . . that her pleasant circumstance is no more a result of her hard work than is the lottery winner's mansion a manifestation of that individual's personal skill at divining what the string of winning number would be. Somebody had to win the lottery; somebody had to be named senior vice president—the dynamics are the same.

Building Personal Responsibility

The manager can increase the probability that the employee will change and resolve a problem if the manager discusses the need for change in terms of the choices the employee makes. We each have the capability for choice; the coaching process makes that capability a part of the system.

It is always appropriate for the manager to consider in advance the various approaches or solutions the employee might use in attempting to resolve a problem. But it is important to recognize that the responsibility for finding a solution to the problem is the employee's, not the manager's. If the manager makes a suggestion that the employee accepts and it subsequently turns out that the suggestion was not effective in solving the problem, the employee can turn back to the manager and say, "See! I did what you told me and it didn't work!" So while the manager may assist the employee by making suggestions or offering guidance, the burden of actually solving the problem is always borne by the individual.

Dealing with Discussion Difficulties

Most discussions about performance—whether Performance Improvement Discussions or formal disciplinary transactions—will proceed without difficulty if the manager prepares effectively for the transaction, focuses the discussion on gaining the employee's agreement to change, and concentrates on the joint objectives of solving the problem and enhancing the relationship. Difficulties, however, are always waiting to challenge even the most experienced manager. Typically these discussion difficulties present themselves as games played by the employee. While the employee may not consciously intend or even be aware that she is attempting to engage the manager in a manipulative game, the fact remains that there are communication games the unwary manager can be sucked into.

Unlike real life games, these treacherous communication games are ones that the manager cannot win. The only way to deal with them is to confront them and move on.

The "Yeahbut" Game

The "Yeahbut" game, first described by psychologist Eric Berne in his book, *Games People Play*, arises when the manager attempts to be helpful to the subordinate by suggesting possible courses of action for the subordinate to take in order to solve the problem the subordinate faces:

Manager: "Sally, you've got to be here on time every day."

Employee: "Yeahbut with six kids to get up in the morning it sure is tough to get to work on time."

Manager: "Well, Sally, maybe if you got your kids up a little earlier in the morning you could get them off to school and then get to work on time."

Employee: "Yeahbut the kids stay up so late it sure is tough to get them up in the morning."

Manager: "Well, Sally, maybe if you put the kids to bed a little earlier at night you could get them up a little earlier in the morning."

Employee: "Yeahbut you know my husband works the second shift and they sure like to see their daddy come home."

Manager: Well, Sal, maybe if . . ."

Employee: Yeahbut . . ."

And it keeps on going. It turns out that for every piece of good advice that the manager has, the employee always has one more "yeahbut." And when the employee has delivered that one last "yeahbut" and the manager is unable to come up with any more good advice, what the employee has done is successfully demonstrate that the problem cannot be solved. "If you," Sally sweetly summarizes, "my boss, my leader, my source of truth and wisdom and light . . . if you can't figure out how to solve this problem, how could you ever expect poor little me to . . . ?"

Whenever you hear the word "yeahbut," recognize that you are being sucked into a game. It is a game that you cannot win. The only escape is agreement. Agree with whatever objection the employee has raised and turn the responsibility back where it belongs:

> *Manager*: "You're right, Sally. That is a real problem. I agree. It would be difficult for me, too. How are you planning to handle that situation so that you can meet your responsibility of being here every day?"

And when Sally responds, "Gee, I don't know," an appropriate response from the manager could be, "Well, Sally, you need to think about that carefully, because I need someone in this job who can be here every day, and I sure hope that person is you. . . ."

The Silence Game

The "silence game" is invoked when the employee chooses not to respond to the manager's attempts to discuss the problem. In some cases, the silence is understandable because—out of apprehension or anxiety—the individual simply becomes so tongue-tied that he cannot speak. The more sinister form of the silence game arises when the employee uses silence as a vehicle for intimidation.

Silence can be used to intimidate. The important question is, Who's going to be intimidated?

There is no reason for the manager to be intimidated by the employee's silence. If the cause of the silence appears to be the employee's anxiety, a pause and a gentle question like, "Are you feeling OK?"

will usually be enough to get the person to respond so that the discussion can continue. But when silence is deliberate and the employee obstinately refuses to respond, a different tack is called for.

"Refusing to engage in a business discussion," or "engaging in inappropriate behavior during a business meeting" are disciplinary offenses that the individual may be confronted with if he obstinately refuses to discuss a problem. In fact, they are a form of insubordination in which the employee is willfully failing to perform a normal part of his job: discussing his performance with his boss.

After one or two questions have gone unanswered and the manager is suspicious that he is encountering an insubordination situation, the following dialogue might well be appropriate:

Manager: "So that's my concern, Bill. I need you to agree that in the future you won't clock out until your shift is officially over."

Employee: [*silence*]

Manager: "Is there a problem, Bill? I need your agreement that you will follow this procedure."

Employee: [*silence*]

Manager: "Bill, if you are refusing to discuss this situation it is a very serious matter. Are you refusing to respond to my request?"

Employee: [*silence*]

Manager: "Bill, I am now giving you a direct order to discuss this situation with me and get it resolved. If you refuse to obey my order, you will be committing an act of insubordination. This is a very serious offense. You will be subject to discharge if you continue to refuse. Are you willing to discuss this situation?"

Employee: [*silence*]

Manager: "Bill, this meeting is over. We will get together later to discuss what has become a very serious matter of insubordination."

At this point the employee should return to the workplace, or perhaps more wisely, be "suspended pending investigation" and advised to leave the workplace immediately. Most organizations would recommend that the security function be called and for the employee to be escorted from the factory or office.

This scenario, proceeding from the employee's original silence through all of his refusals to speak, is rare. Most organizations would consider a Decision Making Leave, the final step of the Discipline Without Punishment system, to be the appropriate response (if they charitably decided not to terminate). Most of the time however, upon being asked if he is specifically *refusing* to speak, an employee will quickly realize that the situation is far more serious than he anticipated and will rapidly explain that he is not refusing. At this point an excellent opportunity presents itself to the manager to engage in a bit of coaching about appropriate organizational behavior at a time when the employee is totally ready to absorb it.

The "I'll Try" Game

The manager asks the subordinate to agree to change and do the job properly. "OK, boss," the subordinate cheerfully responds, "I'll try."

Have you gained an agreement?

Of course you have! The subordinate has agreed to try. And the next time you see her filing her nails and reading a magazine when she should be on the phone with customers, what will her response be? "I tried. . . ."

Trying doesn't count. Only doing what you're paid to do counts. But when the employee responds with either a gay or a grudging "I'll try," realize that you are actually getting close to a legitimate agreement. Parry the "I'll try" response with acceptance ("That's great, Bertha!") and move toward an actual statement of what the employee will do to make the good intention a reality ("I'm glad to hear that and I'm sure that you will try. But what will you actually do to make sure that you'll be successful?").

The Irrelevancy Game

Sooner or later, every manager, no matter how skilled, will get caught in the irrelevancy trap. Here you are, sailing smoothly along in what most managers would find a very difficult conversation, talking comfortably with the employee about how he will redirect his efforts to assure fully acceptable job performance, and then wham! You discover you're in the middle of a discussion of an issue that is absolutely irrelevant to the subject at hand. Here's what usually happens:

Manager: "Wait a minute. That's irrelevant."

Employee: "No, it's not."

Manager: "Yes, it is."

Employee: "No, it's not!"

Manager: "Yes, it is!"

Employee: "NO, IT'S NOT!"

And on and on.

Labeling an irrelevancy as such is unproductive. It only generates arguments. Don't waste your time.

When you realize that you are in the middle of an active discussion concerning an irrelevant topic, the technique to use is, "Dismiss and Redirect." Wait until your counterpart pauses for breath, and then say, "As far as the way they used to handle this situation in your old company is concerned, I'd like to talk about that separately. First, I need for you to agree to come to work every day."

The key words are "separately" and "first." The magic "Dismiss and Redirect" technique can be used anytime your conversational counterpart raises an issue that you want to make go away. You don't say that it's irrelevant or unimportant or unconnected with the matter at hand. Instead, you graciously acknowledge its importance and then, with a sweep of misdirection, consign it to the nether world of irrelevancies and return to the primary issue on your agenda:

"I appreciate your bringing to my attention the fact that the attendance record of other people in the department should be examined, Betty. I'd like to deal with that separately. First, I need your agreement that you will maintain a fully acceptable record."

"It may well be that no one has ever said anything to you before about taking supplies home, Frank, but I'd like to talk about that separately. First, I need for you to empty your pockets . . . "

Note that the term is *separately* and not *later*. *Separately* may well mean "never."

If the employee is raising an issue that could turn out to be important to explore, using the Dismiss and Redirect technique still allows you to accomplish the primary objective of gaining the employee's agreement. Once you have gained the agreement, it is fully appropriate to bring the earlier redirected issue up for current consideration: "Now that we've resolved this problem of shortages, Matthew, I'd like to go back to what you were saying earlier about there being a lot of places where the company's money was flowing away. What did you have in mind when you said that?"

Closing the Discussion

If the conversation has been a Performance Improvement Discussion, simply thank the person for agreeing to correct the situation and express your confidence that the two of you will never need to talk about the matter again. However, if the discussion is a formal disciplinary transaction, the manager must take two additional steps:

1. Advise the employee that it is a formal disciplinary transaction.
2. Advise the employee which step of the Discipline Without Punishment system is being taken.

The manager should also make sure that the employee understands just what it means to be on a formal level of disciplinary action. He should review the company's policies regarding disciplinary action with the person and explain any procedural guidelines. The conversation might sound like this:

Manager: "I'm glad you've agreed to solve this problem, Cathy, and I'm sure we won't ever need to talk about it again. Since this is the third time you and I have had to talk about this matter, this conversation is a formal Reminder 1. It's the first step of the company's discipline procedure. Do you know what that means?"

Employee: "Well, not really. It's not good, is it?"

Manager: "No, it's not good, but it doesn't automatically become part of your personnel record. It is the first formal level of our Discipline Without Punishment procedure. I will be documenting what we have talked about today, along with your agreement to change, but I'll be keeping those records here in the department. Nothing will go into your permanent file unless we have to talk again. But I don't think we'll need to talk about this again, will we, Cathy?"

Employee: "No, Mr. Navarro. I'm sure we won't."

Manager: "Me too, Cathy. It will officially remain active for six months, which means that if another problem comes up we will consider this incident in deciding what to do about the next one. If there are no further problems, in six months it will be dead and will be taken out of the file. If you'll make a note to talk to me six months from today, I'll make arrangements to have this deactivated. Is that fair?"

Employee: "Sure. Is that all?"

Manager: "That's it, Cathy. Let's get back to work."

Whether the discussion is a Performance Improvement Discussion or a formal disciplinary transaction, the manager's final comments should be directed toward building a positive expectation of improvement.

When the manager has gained the employee's agreement, discussed and decided upon the action the individual will take to solve the problem, advised the employee whether or not the discussion is a formal disciplinary transaction, and expressed a personal belief that this will be the last time they will ever have to address the matter, the Discuss step has been completed.

Notes

1. Carroll R. Daugherty, *Grief Bros. Cooperage Corp.*, quoted in James R. Redeker, *Discipline: Policies and Procedures* (Washington, D.C.: The Bureau of National Affairs, Inc., 1983). pp. 15-18.
2. Ibid.

PART III

DISCIPLINE

WITHOUT

PUNISHMENT

FORMAL DISCIPLINARY ACTION

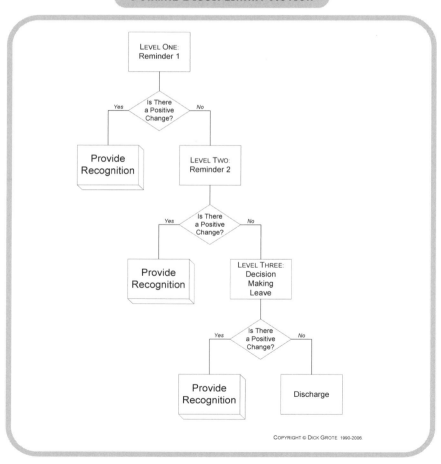

CHAPTER 6

The Mechanics of Discipline Without Punishment

Chapter 5 concentrates on how to conduct an effective discussion with an individual to bring about a change in that person's performance or behavior. The techniques I describe for successful problem-solving meetings will work whether the transaction is a serious conversation aimed at preventing the need for formal disciplinary action (a Performance Improvement Discussion) or a formal step of the Discipline Without Punishment procedure (a Reminder 1/Reminder 2/Decision Making Leave discussion). This chapter explores in detail the actual procedures and mechanics for conducting effective Performance Improvement Discussions and disciplinary discussions at the Reminder 1 or Reminder 2 level. The Decision Making Leave (DML) is a unique step, which we discuss separately in Chapter 7.

To begin, let's look at the most important similarities and differences between Performance Improvement Discussions and formal disciplinary transactions (Reminders 1 and 2 and DMLs). While Performance Improvement Discussions are part of the overall Discipline Without Punishment methodology, they are not formal steps of disciplinary action. (We use them to prevent having to take disciplinary action.) Both Performance Improvement Discussions and discipline steps are carefully planned, initiated by the immediate supervisor, and have the same goal—getting the employee to agree to change.

But there are some significant differences. Disciplinary action usually requires the supervisor to get someone else's OK before proceeding and a witness is often present. While for Performance Improvement Discussions it's certainly a good idea to conduct a full investigation in advance and to document what was discussed after the meeting is over. When formal disciplinary action is taken, those actions are mandatory. Finally, there's usually a limit on how many Reminder 1s or Reminder 2s an employee can get before moving on to the next more serious step. There's no limit on the number of Performance Improvement Discussions a supervisor can conduct. A summary of the similarities and differences is shown in Figure 6-1.

In reviewing the procedures for each of these steps, I am assuming that the problem being dealt with is one that it is appropriate to start with a Performance Improvement Discussion and then move in a step-by-step way through the discipline system if it is not corrected. While this is true of the great majority of problems that managers in organizations encounter, managers also have to deal with serious issues that are too threatening or potentially damaging to justify starting with a Performance Improvement Discussion or even a Reminder 1. For these situations the appropriate response to a first offense would be a Reminder 2 or even a Decision Making Leave.

There are also those offenses so grave that the employee has not earned the right to rehabilitation through the organization's disciplinary procedures. For these offenses, like theft or assaulting a customer or coworker, termination is the most appropriate response even when no previous disciplinary action has ever been taken. (In Chapter 10 we review the offenses that are usually considered sufficiently serious as to justify skipping the early steps and beginning with a Reminder 2 or a Decision Making Leave. We also review the offenses that usually warrant termination for a first offense, and how that termination should be handled.)

For each procedure, I explain what to do *before* the meeting, *during* the meeting, and *after* the meeting.

Figure 6-1. Performance improvement discussion and formal steps of disciplinary action compared.

Similarities:

	Performance Improvement Discussion	Reminder 1 Reminder 2 Decision Making Leave
Part of DWP system?	Yes	Yes
Purpose of discussion?	Gain agreement to correct problem	Gain agreement to correct problem
Planned in advance?	Yes	Yes
Initiator	Immediate supervisor	Immediate supervisor
Conducted in private?	Yes	Yes

Differences:

	Performance Improvement Discussion	Reminder 1 Reminder 2 Decision Making Leave
Formal level of disciplinary action?	No	Yes
Investigation required before taking action?	No	Yes
Documentation required?	No	Yes
Witness required?	No	Frequently (policies vary)
Is there a limit on the number an employee may receive?	No	Yes
Is advance approval required?	No	Usually

Procedures: Performance Improvement Discussion

If this is the first time that you and the employee have had to have a serious discussion about a problem (either because it has just come up or because earlier casual conversations have not been effective), you'll need to make notes to help you stay on track during the meeting and be sure of a successful outcome. The Discussion Worksheet: Pre-Meeting Checklist, which indicates all of the information you'll need to jot down in order to be fully prepared, is included as Appendix A at the end of the book.

As you'll see, the Discussion Worksheet includes space to indicate the category of problem (attendance, performance, or conduct); dates of previous conversations; the specific desired and actual performance; a brief summary of the good business reasons why it must be solved; and the consequences the employee will face if he chooses not to change.

The worksheet also provides the "Five Classic Questions" discussed in Chapter 5. It's a good idea to consider and actually check each of the five boxes to indicate that the issue has been considered and the answer is *yes*.

Finally, there's a place to indicate whether the action you're planning to take is a Performance Improvement Discussion or whether it is one of the formal steps of Discipline Without Punishment.

During the Meeting

As soon as the employee comes into the room or office, begin the meeting by immediately getting to the issue at hand. Use the model described in Chapter 5 to begin the conversation. (Say, "George, I have a problem," review the actual and desired performance, then invite the employee to respond by saying, "Tell me about it," or making a similar statement.)

In listening to what the individual says, be sensitive to any indicators that the problem may result from either a deficiency in knowledge (where additional training or skill-building may be more appropriate), or a deficiency in execution (where job engineering efforts may be required). Listen also to determine whether the cause of the problem might be a situation best addressed through your Employee Assistance Program.

Tell the individual the specific change you are seeking and gain the employee's agreement to solve the problem. The most useful and straightforward way to gain someone's agreement, of course, is simply to ask for it: "Bill, I need for you to agree that you will always respond to customer inquiries within two days." Or, "Elizabeth, it is important that no customer be kept waiting if at all avoidable. May I have your agreement that whenever you are doing paperwork and a customer comes up, that you will pause in your paperwork and attend to the customer's needs?"

Once the employee has agreed to perform properly in the future, feel free to discuss any significant issues that the individual may have raised in the course of the earlier discussion when the primary agenda was the seeking of agreement. Discuss the specific action that the employee will take to solve the problem and, if appropriate, the action that you as the manager will take to assist in the effort.

Close the meeting by creating a "self-fulfilling prophecy" that this will be the last time that the two of you will ever need to discuss the matter. If necessary, explain that the discussion has been a Performance Improvement Discussion and not a formal disciplinary transaction. Shake hands and get back to work.

After the Meeting

While it is still fresh in your mind, make some notes to summarize the discussion. Record the date of the session, the employee's exact agreement, and any statements the employee made that may be useful later on. If the employee agreed to take certain actions, make a note of the specific commitment the individual made. If you agreed to do anything, record that, too. File these notes wherever you keep other department personnel information. The Discussion Worksheet: Post-Meeting Summary is included as Appendix B.

After the meeting, follow up on the conversation to make sure that the problem has been solved. After an appropriate amount of time has passed without another instance of the problem, recognize the employee through a discussion on the subject or with an informal note that you have recognized and appreciate the correction.

I have just summarized the step-by-step procedures for having a Performance Improvement Discussion—a serious and carefully planned transaction that is not a formal step of disciplinary action. The Reminder 1 and Reminder 2 transactions are formal disciplinary steps.

Procedures: Reminder 1

As I review the procedures for these steps, you'll be surprised at how little difference there is between a Performance Improvement Discussion and a formal step of disciplinary action. And the tone of the conversation is identical in each: business-like, serious, calm, and respectful.

Before the Meeting

The procedures for the Reminder 1 are almost identical to those for the Performance Improvement Discussion (and will be virtually the same as those for the Reminder 2.)

Since this is now a formal disciplinary transaction, it is necessary to conduct a full investigation before beginning the disciplinary transaction. Conducting "a full and fair investigation" isn't burdensome. It simply involves asking and answering yes to the "Five Classic Questions" described in Chapter 5.

The same information that you gathered for the Performance Improvement Discussion is needed before conducting a Reminder 1 or Reminder 2 transaction: category of problem, desired and actual performance, adverse effects, logical consequences. One additional area may also be appropriate now: If you had an earlier conversation with the employee about the issue and were successful in gaining the individual's agreement to solve the problem, you will want to raise the employee's failure to live up to the agreement for discussion in this meeting. Be sure to note the exact agreement that was made previously.

Many organizations require the supervisor to get approval from his immediate supervisor or department head before conducting the Reminder 1 discussion. Some require human resources to be either advised or to approve in advance before the Reminder 1 discussion takes place. Be sure to review the situation with the appropriate individuals before beginning the conversation.

Should a witness be present? Some organizations require it; others leave it to the supervisor's discretion. As we've discussed, a witness to the transaction is particularly appropriate if there is any concern that the disciplinary discussion may lead to a violent reaction, if the individual is likely to deny that an agreement was made or even that the conversation took place, if the presence of a second member of management is needed to reinforce the importance of getting the problem solved, or if there is reason to believe that a false charge of sexual harassment or other type of improper behavior could be made in retaliation for a disciplinary step being taken.

If the employee is represented by a union, the shop steward or other union representative should be asked to attend, and the meeting should not begin without the employee's representative being present.

Ask the individual and the representative, if present, to come into your office. If your boss or other management witness is present, make introductions so that everyone knows who is present and what their purpose in attending the meeting is.

During the Meeting

As with any meeting on an important business issue, get right to the point. This is particularly important when there are several people present besides just the supervisor and the employee. There is no reason to vary from the approach used to open the Performance Improvement Discussion of saying, "I've got a problem and I need your help in getting it solved," reviewing the desired and actual performance or the rule violation, and then asking the individual to respond.

The balance of the meeting follows the procedures for the Performance Improvement Discussion:

- Listen to what the employee has to say to make sure that there is no reason not to proceed with the formal Reminder 1.
- Review the previous discussions (both casual conversations and any more serious coaching sessions) that you and the employee have had about the situation.
- If a previous discussion resulted in the employee's agreement to correct the situation, indicate that you are concerned not only with the continuation of the original problem but also with the employee's failure to live up to the agreement that he made.
- Advise the individual of the specific performance change that is required and confirm that the employee knows exactly what is expected.
- Gain the employee's agreement to solve the problem.
- Advise the employee that this conversation is a formal Reminder 1.
- Bring the meeting to a close by communicating a positive expectation of change.

One common problem at the Reminder 1 level is the supervisor's failure to state directly that the discussion is a formal disciplinary transaction. Here's how this problem arises. The supervisor and the employee at this point have discussed a business problem in a businesslike way and have reached agreement about its solution. Eager to maintain the good relationship, the supervisor, consciously or inadvertently, may decide not to spoil things by announcing that the discussion has moved beyond an informal Performance Improvement Discussion and is now a formal disciplinary transaction. Believing that the discussion has had the intended effect, that the employee will indeed correct the situation and that they will never again need to discuss the issue, he fails to advise the employee that the discussion is part of the organization's formal discipline procedure.

Sometimes he will be correct. When he is, he will have made a wise decision in veering away at the last minute from calling the discussion a formal discipline step.

Too often, however, the plan goes awry. The employee fails to deliver on his promise and the two of them meet again. Now the supervisor is angry. The problem has continued and the employee has failed to live up to his commitment to change. Worse, he feels taken advantage of. Having given the employee a break, he feels he has been deceived and dealt with in bad faith.

He wants to move to the Reminder 2 or directly to the Decision Making Leave. Unfortunately, he has no justification for either, since the Reminder 1 transaction actually has never taken place.

Because he did not advise the employee that the earlier conversation was a Reminder 1, it was not. It was just another failed coaching session, and there is no justification for moving from a Performance Improvement Discussion to the second step of the discipline system without using the first step first.

"But I did give him a Reminder 1," the supervisor protests. "I followed all the procedures for the Reminder 1 step. The only thing I didn't do was say the literal words, 'This is a Reminder 1.'"

And because he did not say the literal words, "This is a Reminder 1," therefore it was not. An employee must be advised if a transaction is, in fact, a step of the discipline process.

After the Meeting

The key difference in post-meeting activity between the Reminder 1 and the Performance Improvement Discussion involves documentation. While it is desirable for a record to be made of all informal conversations, it is not required that they be formally documented. A Reminder 1, or any formal disciplinary discussion, must be documented.

The simplest way to document a disciplinary discussion at the Reminder 1 level is to use the Discussion Worksheet: Post-Meeting Summary, shown in Appendix B.

Most companies keep this form within the department and do not forward any copy to the central personnel records. Retaining the Reminder 1 documentation within the walls of the department provides several benefits. Most performance problems that get to the Reminder 1 stage are solved at that stage, so there is no reason for human resources to become involved unless the problem continues and the disciplinary response escalates. In that case, a copy of the Reminder 1 worksheet will simply be attached to HR's copy of the Reminder 2 memo to provide a complete record. Also, by keeping the Reminder 1 documentation within the department, the supervisor can advise the employee that nothing will go into the individual's permanent personnel record unless they have to move to the next step of the system. This can serve as a powerful incentive to change.

Procedures: Reminder 2

As before, the supervisor conducts an investigation and completes the worksheet listing the critical information required both for discussion during the meeting and the subsequent documentation.

Before the Meeting

Since the worksheet the supervisor filled out in preparation for the previous Reminder 1 will probably be available, most of the information should be readily on hand.

Virtually every organization requires that before initiating a Reminder 2 disciplinary discussion, the supervisor get approval from one higher level of management in her own department as well as the concurrence of the human resources function. The purpose of requiring approvals is not to get the permission of personnel and senior management but, rather, to ensure that similar problems are being dealt with in a reasonably similar manner throughout the organization. With the necessary approvals obtained, the meeting may begin.

During the Meeting

The manner and approach of the supervisor is no different from earlier transactions. She is serious, calm, dignified, businesslike, and unruffled regardless of what the employee's behavior may be. She is a person with a mission who will be undeterred from reaching her objective: to review the existence of a problem with the individual who is creating that problem; to explain why it is a problem and what the logical consequences of failure to correct it will be; and then to secure the employee's agreement that he will correct the situation and return to a fully acceptable level of performance. The only indicator that this session is more serious than earlier conversations is the supervisor's reference to previous discussions and the employee's failure to do what he said he would do.

Since previous discussions have not produced the required results, it's appropriate now for the supervisor to spend more time discussing the specific things the employee will actually do to solve the problem once and for all. Previously she may simply have accepted the employee's stated agreement as sufficient; now she will want to probe behind the words. When the employee proposes an action that might correct the situation, the manager will press the employee, firmly but respectfully, to make good on his intentions:

Manager: ". . . So what will you actually do to get here on time every day, Carlos, other than just try harder?"

Employee: "Well, like I said, the big problem is my car. The only reason that I'm ever late is that sometimes it doesn't start, or it gives out on the way."

Manager: "So what are you going to do about that?"

Employee: "It's basically OK. Mostly it just needs a tune-up and new tires."

Manager: "So what are you going to do?"

Employee: "Well, I guess I'll get a tune-up and new tires."

Manager: "That makes sense. When do you plan to do that?"

Employee: "Well, gee, I don't know. I don't have a lot of time and money's kind of tight right now."

Manager: "I understand. What do you think you'll do?"

Employee: "Well, I could go ahead and get the tune-up done. I could get some of the parts myself and my brother and I could do most of the work this weekend."

Manager: "That seems like a good idea. Will you actually do it?"

Employee: "Yeah. I have to do it. I have to get my car back running right."

Manager: "Good. What will you do about the tires?"

Employee: "I don't know. I can't afford to get new tires. They're real expensive and I'm tight right now. What do you think I should do?"

Manager: "I don't know, Carlos. What I do know is that if you can't come to work every day on time, you can't work here. We need somebody who can be here every day."

Employee: "Yeah, I guess you're right. But I can't help it if I get a flat."

Manager: "Well, let's be clear about that, Carlos. It is your responsibility to be here on time every day. And when you're not here, it really doesn't make any difference whether it's a flat tire or anything else. (Pause) What are you going to do?"

Employee: "I'm going to get new tires."

Manager: "How will you do that?"

Employee: "Well, I'll see if I can get retreads, and if I can't, I know I can borrow some of the money I need from my sister."

Manager: "Will that solve the problem?"

Employee: "Yeah. I won't be late again."

While we won't know until later whether Carlos will, in fact, get his car tuned up and put new tires on it (and, more important, whether he will then start arriving at work on time every day), the supervisor has successfully moved Carlos away from just stating good intentions and into making specific plans. Depending on the situation and the individual, even more planning, problem solving, and goal setting might be appropriate.

Throughout the transaction, whether at the Reminder 2 level or any earlier one, the supervisor needs to be clear not only about the expected standard of performance, but also the employee's responsibility to arrange the circumstances of his life so that he can meet that standard. In the preceding dialogue, the supervisor did not take the responsibility away from Carlos by offering up suggestions for him to reject. Instead she agreed with Carlos that Carlos was facing a problem. But when asked for advice she appropriately said, "I don't know. . . . What I do know is that if you can't come to work every day on time, you can't work here. We need somebody who can be here every day."

When the supervisor has gained the employee's agreement and discussed exactly what action the individual will take to assure a permanent correction of the situation, she must advise the employee that the discussion is a Reminder 2—the second level of the Discipline Without Punishment procedure.

After the Meeting

The greatest difference between the Reminder 1 and the Reminder 2 is the documentation of the two steps. The Reminder 1 is documented by the supervisor's simply completing a discussion worksheet and placing it the department file. To document the Reminder 2, the supervisor should also complete the discussion summary form, but the primary documentation of the transaction is a memo confirming the discussion and the employee's commitment to correct the problem.

It's important to use a memo and not a preprinted form. When companies use a warning notice form, they usually require that it be completed before the meeting. This procedure reduces the chance that meaningful discussion will take place once the employee discovers that the form has already been filled out.

Here's a more serious problem. Effective disciplinary documentation provides complete information about the problem itself, the history of the problem, and, most important, the discussion that occurred between the employee and the manager about the problem. If the manager writes the notice before talking to the employee, it is impossible to record any aspects of the discussion. The manager may later come back and add to the notice some comments about whatever the employee said, but, for the most part, once the manager has "written him up," whatever has been written remains unchanged.

Wait until the meeting is over. Then write the employee a memo summarizing everything that was said and the fact that the meeting was a Reminder 2—the second step of the Discipline Without Punishment process. The memo should be written by the supervisor and written to the employee, not *about* the employee. Make sure the following information is included:

- The names of the supervisor, the employee, and any witnesses who were present.

- The date on which the discussion took place (and the location, if significant).

- The specific problem that caused the transaction to occur.

- A record of all previous conversations about the problem and the dates on which each of those conversations occurred. This record should include formal disciplinary conversations, Performance Improvement Discussions, and casual conversations (even though no record of the conversation was made). If the individual received an earlier Reminder 1 for this problem, or if the person received this Reminder 2 because he was on an active Reminder 1 for an unrelated problem, this fact should be directly stated.

- A statement, in all detail required, of what continuing problems have been experienced since the earlier conversations took place.

- A statement that the situation must be corrected (not "improved").

- A statement of the specific change that must be made.

- A statement of the fact that failure to correct the problem may lead to more serious disciplinary action.

- A statement that in addition to solving the immediate problem, the organization expects the employee to maintain an acceptable level of performance in every area of his job.

- A record of the agreement made by the employee to correct the problem.

- A record of any action the employee agreed to take in order to bring about the correction.

- A closing statement that expresses the supervisor's belief that the problem will, in fact, be corrected and that the employee will perform properly in the future.

There is a great deal of information to be communicated. Using the preceding checklist to prepare the documentation memo will make writing the memo easier, ensure that it incorporates all required information, and prevent inappropriate information from slipping in.

Appendix C is an example of a Reminder 2 memo.

Reviewing the Memo with the Employee

In companies that use the traditional progressive-discipline system, the supervisor writes the warning notice to the employee in advance of the discussion, issues the warning to the employee during the meeting, and files the copies after the meeting. In the Discipline Without Punishment procedure, the disciplinary transaction is documented by writing a memo to the employee summarizing the conversation. Since this memo is written after the meeting has been completed, the manager needs to meet with the employee again to review the Reminder 2 memo.

Many managers are initially reluctant to invest the time required for a second meeting. Why can't this memo, like most memos, simply be delivered to the employee through the organization's regular transmission process? they ask. While this would be the most convenient approach, most companies that implement the Discipline Without Punishment system ask the manager to hold a short second meeting to review the memo with the employee.

While a second meeting does increase the total amount of time devoted to the Reminder 2 transaction, that disadvantage is overcome by the benefits provided. First, managers actually conduct few Reminder 2 transactions in the course of a year. Asking the manager to hold a second meeting to review the memo will not significantly increase his workload.

Second, the meeting is short and tightly focused. The sole purpose is to give the employee the memo, respond to any questions, and reconfirm the agreement that the problem will be solved. More than five minutes is too long.

This meeting may be one of the most important a manager can have with a subordinate in terms of its ability to significantly influence performance. It gives the employee the opportunity to ask any questions that may have come up in the day or two since the initial meeting was held, and allows the manager to explain the specific policy and procedural details of the Discipline Without Punishment process when the employee is likely to be less defensive. Most important, it provides an opportunity for the disciplinary documentation to be corrected if the manager has not accurately captured what was said during the meeting.

Should the Employee Sign?

In all of management, there is probably no piece of advice that is repeated unquestioningly more often than the admonition to always have the employee sign the document. Preprinted warning notice forms invariably contain a space for the employee's signature; every book that reviews the basic steps of the progressive-discipline procedure mandates that the employee be required to sign.

This is another area where the conventional wisdom about discipline is wrong.

Why do we ask the employee to sign? Managers invariably respond to that familiar question with a well-drilled schoolbook answer: "To acknowledge receipt."

But ask them when that acknowledgment of receipt will be valuable and they stumble. It takes some grappling to come up with the precise answer: In the event that the employee ever asserts that he did not see the document, his signature proves that he's lying.

When will that event ever arise? It turns out that in order for the employee's signature on the disciplinary documentation to have any value, the following scenario must play out in its entirety. The individual must continue his misbehavior through the point of a Decision Making Leave and then be fired. He must then challenge his termination through an arbitration or legal proceeding. The matter must then proceed to a formal hearing or trial without earlier settlement. At the trial or hearing the employee's sole defense must be that the incident never happened. The company, he must claim, is making it all up. It never happened. They put this in my file without telling me.

But this just doesn't happen. Only some of the people who get Reminder 2s continue their misbehavior and move on to Decision Making Leaves. Most clean up their act and never encounter disciplinary problems again. Only some of the people who get Decision Making Leaves decide not to live up to their commitment and get terminated. Only some of those who get terminated take their unhappiness all the way to arbitration or a court proceeding.

And even then, almost never does a terminated employee argue that the incident never happened and that management put the warning notice in his file when he wasn't looking. He argues instead that it was undeserved. "Well, sure, I got this thing," he will admit. "But I shouldn't have. I didn't deserve it. They treated me different than other people. They singled me out because I was black/female/handicapped/Jewish."

The only value that the employee's signature provides is the proof that the transaction did, in fact, take place. But employees almost never argue that it didn't take place, particularly because the supervisor is usually quite capable of testifying as to exactly what was said during the meeting and confirming that the discussion did, in fact, occur. Instead, they will acknowledge that they got the warning notice but that it was inappropriate or unfair—a much stronger argument than the mere pretense that the conversation never happened. The signature has virtually no value.

"I have no problem with abolishing the preprinted warning notice and replacing it with the use of a memo directed to the employee," says Atlanta labor attorney Jim Wimberly. "While I have had employees deny that they have received certain warnings, I rarely, if ever, have had an employee deny that he received a memo directed to him for him to keep."

But ask a manager what the employee's reaction is when you ask him to sign the warning notice. It just pisses them off, they'll tell you. Most of the time people refuse to sign.

And what do you do then?

They explain that when the employee refuses to sign, as he usually does, they write down that the employee refused to sign.

Your case is no stronger. When the employee later claims that the transaction never happened, he will point out that the writing on the form saying that he refused to sign is certainly not his, and that not only did the company put it in his file without his knowing about it, they also wrote down that he refused to sign something that he had never seen.

Reflect on what happens when you ask the employee to sign the disciplinary documentation. At this point you have completed the Reminder 2 discussion with the individual. Because you followed all of the procedures we have described, and because you dealt with that individual as a mature and responsible adult and conducted your discussion in a dignified and businesslike way, you have gained the employee's agreement to solve a problem. When you met with the employee and asked him to review the memo to make sure that it reasonably reflected the discussion that the two of you had, you again communicated your expectation that the problem was now a thing of the past. If you now present him with a pen and demand that he sign it, what are you saying to that person?

What the demand to sign the notice actually says to the employee is that you believe him to be a liar. The demand for his signature implies that even though he has agreed to solve the problem and correct the situation, he won't. You are suggesting that you are worried that he is going to continue his misbehavior and receive a Decision Making Leave, and that following the Leave he will again perform unacceptably and be terminated. You are insinuating that you know that he will challenge the termination and that when the two of you are standing there, side by side, in front of the judge or arbitrator or hearing officer, that he will lie about the fact that the two of you are talking about the problem right now. And, therefore, your request proclaims, I am asking you to sign this form so that I can protect myself against you.

Is that the message we want to send to the people who look to us for leadership?

I submit that it is not. I submit that there is a far more effective way to handle the issue of whether the employee should be required to sign the disciplinary notice. I propose that we abolish the progressive-discipline requirement that employees be compelled to sign the documentation.

What should we do? When the employee has read the memo and agreed that it basically reflects what was said in the meeting and then asks whether he now must sign it, I would have the manager look him in the eye and say, "John, are you a man of your word?"

I would have the manager wait until John replies that indeed he is.

"I know you are, John," I would have the manager respond. "So if you tell me that this problem is solved for good and we won't ever have to talk about it again, your word is good enough for me. You don't have to sign a thing."

Fanciful? Capricious? Perhaps. And while the scenario of the manager's looking John in the eye, asking him if he is indeed a man of his word, and then stating that his word is sufficient, may rarely be enacted verbatim, eliminating the hollow requirement that the manager compel John's signature will not lessen in the slightest the company's ability to defend its action in the rare case that the presence or absence of the signature ever becomes an issue.

Even when our experience with the individual suggests that we are dealing with someone who is unlikely to solve the problem and will not hesitate to lie if it serves his advantage, requiring the signature on the Reminder 2 memo still provides little value. We still have the Decision Making Leave step in our arsenal. If there is any concern that the employee will not live up to his commitment following the Decision Making Leave and will prevaricate when asked about the history of events that resulted in his discharge, we may then decide to require the signature. But the better job we can do at putting the problem to rest at the Reminder 2 stage, the less chance there is that the issue will ever escalate. And eliminating the signature requirement is one small but significant way.

CHAPTER 7

Decision Making Leave

Of all the elements of Discipline Without Punishment, certainly the one that attracts the most attention is the final step of the system—the paid Decision Making Leave (DML).

Managers who can comfortably accept the idea of dealing with employees who create problems as responsible adults during the first steps of the process sometimes have difficulty extending that same philosophy to the last step. The idea of a paid disciplinary suspension invariably takes some explaining.

Whatever the final step of a discipline system is, it must meet two requirements. First, it must be sufficiently tough so as to produce the required change in the individual's behavior that less serious actions have failed to do. It must also be a sufficiently dramatic gesture so that should the individual's employment later have to be terminated because of his failure to change, any third party would agree that the person got sufficient notice that his job was at risk and that the company had done everything it could to try to turn the individual around. While an unpaid suspension of several days is both tough and dramatic, we know that punishment frequently brings far more problems

144

than it solves. While companies have explored other alternatives, there is no more effective final-step technique than the use of a Decision Making Leave.

Other Alternatives

There are three traditional alternatives to Decision Making Leave: probation, performance improvement plans, and a final warning.

Probation?

A probationary period is the least effective of all final step tactics. In most cases, placing an employee on probation for ninety days is simply a way to avoid dealing with the problem directly. Rarely does the employee or the supervisor take it seriously. Most of the time it's an empty gesture aimed more at providing the appearance of action than in actually confronting the problem in a forthright way. And there's a real risk with using a probationary period as a final disciplinary step— employees who are placed on probation may feel that they have been given license by the organization to continue their misbehavior for another ninety days.

Performance Improvement Plans?

Some organizations have had some success by asking the supervisor to work together with the employee to create a Performance Improvement Plan (PIP). While the idea of supervisor and employee working together to develop these action plans is attractive, there are several problems with this approach. First, it's appropriate only for those problems that fall into the performance category. Creating a PIP seems ludicrous for an employee who decides to smoke in a restricted area or violates one of the other rules of the organization. PIPs for attendance issues are equally inappropriate.

Another problem with using a PIP approach as a final-step tactic is that most of the actions that would make up a PIP have already been taken. If the supervisor has been clear about the exact gap between desired and actual performance, and if she had met her responsibilities of providing training, arranging appropriate consequences, providing feedback, and removing obstacles, she would have already created a PIP in everything but name.

Finally, while the use of a Performance Improvement Plan can be integrated with a more formal discipline procedure when it is appropriate (for example, when the problem involves an employee's deficiency in maintaining acceptable quantity or quality of production), the use of a PIP by itself is insufficient as a final discipline strategy. It fails to communicate in unmistakable terms the fact that the current situation is intolerable and that the consequence of failure to correct the problem will be the individual's termination.

A Final Warning?

Using a final warning as the discipline system's final step avoids losing the employee's services during the suspension period. Production, therefore, is not disrupted with other employees needing to be redeployed to cover for the absence. But earlier warnings to this individual about the need for change have not been successful: What evidence is there that more of the same would be any different?

Worse, a final warning as a last step of discipline fails to meet a critical criterion. At the final step of a discipline procedure there must be a dramatic gesture that will unmistakably communicate to the individual that the company is serious about the fact that the situation can not continue. Only a suspension from work can prove, not just to the employee himself but also to any third party who might later review our actions, that the end of the road has at last been reached.

A Tough-Minded Approach

At first the notion of a paid disciplinary suspension seems ridiculously soft at a point when a tough-minded approach is required. It turns out that it is the traditional unpaid suspension that is, in fact, excessively tender.

Here's why. The traditional disciplinary layoff without pay is certainly punishing. But is it a genuinely tough-minded and uncompromising response to an employee's unacceptable behavior? No, it's not.

While a suspension without pay is certainly distasteful for both the supervisor and the employee, the organization is asking almost nothing of the employee except that he serve out his time and not get caught repeating the misbehavior. With the Decision Making Leave, although the individual is being paid for the day he is away from work making his decision, he is also being held to a far higher standard. Returning to work is no longer merely a matter of serving out his sentence. He is now confronted with a far tougher company response to his failure to meet standards. In order to return to his job he has to make an active decision to commit to fully acceptable performance and advise his boss that that is the decision he has made.

Just serving one's time, while somewhat embarrassing and perhaps financially taxing, is not particularly demanding. But to have to spend a day thinking about one's future and then stand in front of one's boss and commit to fully acceptable performance—now there is a tough response.

Procedures: Decision Making Leave

In this section we discuss all the steps involved before, during, and after the meeting to schedule the leave.

Before the Meeting

As in the previous steps of the system, once the supervisor determines that the final step of the Discipline Without Punishment process is appropriate, he completes the worksheet recording the actual and desired performance, the adverse effects of the problem, and the logical consequences if the employee fails to change. At this point, since the Decision Making Leave is the final step of the system, the most significant consequence is, of course, termination.

Every organization that has adopted Discipline Without Punishment requires approval by both a senior line manager and the head of the human resources function before the step is initiated. If a single serious incident precipitates the Decision Making Leave, the supervisor should advise the employee at the time of the incident that this is a serious situation and they will need to discuss it. Since senior management has not yet reviewed and approved the Decision Making Leave, the supervisor needs to advise the individual that he will let her know when they will meet. If the employee can continue to work without presenting any risk to the organization or fellow workers, she may be allowed to continue working while the deliberation process is completed. If there is risk present, she should be suspended pending investigation and told that she will be advised when to return.

More often the precipitating event is not a single calamitous outburst of misbehavior. Instead it is a final straw in a continuing series of minor failures to meet the company's expectations following the Reminder 2. In this case the supervisor, aware that a Decision Making Leave may be forthcoming, has the time to discuss the anticipated need to take the final step with senior members of the organization.

Having secured the necessary approvals, the supervisor must determine how he will cover the employee's work while she is away on the leave. In some cases it will be merely a matter of a minor backlog accumulating; in other cases a major revision to the work schedule may be necessary.

Scheduling the Leave

To what extent should the timing of the leave be adjusted to fit the convenience of the organization? Two guidelines apply here: First, the employee's absence on Decision Making Leave should result in as little organizational disruption as possible. Second, the leave should occur as soon as possible after the precipitating event.

Most of the time the incident that causes the organization to decide to impose a DML and the beginning of the leave itself will occur on the same day. The employee commits the culminating offense, the supervisor rounds up the necessary approvals and plans for work coverage, and by the end of the day the supervisor holds the conversation with the employee and then sends him home to think it over.

Sometimes organizations aren't that lucky. It may be that there is serious deliberation required to determine whether the employee's actions do, in fact, merit moving to the final step. This is particularly true when several employees have been involved in a minor incident of misbehavior. For all the others the normal organizational response would be a Performance Improvement Discussion, or, at most, a Reminder 1. But the individual in question had recently received a Reminder 2 that is still active. Determining the wisest approach in this case may require several heads to sleep on it overnight.

A more difficult decision arises when the need for a DML is clear but the timing is impossible. If Sally, who last week received a Reminder 2 for smoking in a restricted area, is again seen smoking in the same place, the appropriateness of a DML is unarguable. But this week is annual inventory, and Sally is the only inventory clerk who understands the whole system and can serve as a trainer to others.

One approach would be to bite the bullet and place Sally on Decision Making Leave immediately, recognizing that somehow the organization would find a way to deal with her absence if she happened to call in sick that day or get hit by a truck (and at least this way there is a little forewarning). Alternatively the supervisor could have the conversation with Sally and advise her that she will be placed on a Decision Making Leave on _____ (the first workable day that her presence can be spared).

Is the Decision Making Leave a Reward?

A separate issue involves scheduling the DML day to avoid making the day an apparent benefit for the employee. This concern arises when an employee commits an offense that triggers the supervisor's decision to place the employee on a DML. But it's Thursday morning, the supervisor frets. If I place him on Decision Making Leave today, he's not only going to have tomorrow off with pay, but a long weekend as well. Should I juggle the Decision Making Leave transaction in order to prevent the DML day being part of a weekend?

In a word, no.

Behind this question is the lingering remnant of the hard-to-shake misunderstanding that somehow the Decision Making Leave is a form of reward. What the person who asks this question fails to realize is that if the DML day happens to abut a weekend, its impact is even greater. Instead of having only one day where the employee's thoughts will be concentrated on the upcoming meeting where the decision to stay or quit will have to be announced, the individual now faces three days under the gun. The Decision Making Leave is not an additional paid holiday. A Tampa Electric Company employee who returned from Decision Making Leave commented, "Believe me, brother, that was no vacation!"

The only workable way to schedule the DML is to hold the meeting as soon as possible following the triggering incident. As soon as the meeting is over, the employee leaves the premises and is on Decision Making Leave, at full pay, for the balance of that day and for the next regularly scheduled work day.

If that day happens to be a Monday or Friday, so be it. Only if the day abuts an employee's regularly scheduled vacation would it be wise to consciously reschedule the day, not because the DML would extend the employee's vacation, but, out of charity and compassion, to eliminate the anxiety that a two-week-long Decision Making Leave would produce!

The fact is, however, that people don't get placed on Decision Making Leaves on the spur of the moment. It may be that the supervisor has to check her records about what steps have previously been taken to confirm that a DML is now the appropriate action to take. Or the supervisor may have to review the situation with her boss or HR representative to make sure that placing this individual on a DML is reasonably consistent with the action that has previously been taken with other employees who have committed similar offenses.

In addition, the company's procedure is likely to require the advance approval of several individuals before an employee is placed on a Decision Making Leave. One or two of those individuals may not be immediately available.

Finally, it may be that the individual has committed the offense that calls for a DML at a critically important time of the company's business cycle, a time when all hands absolutely must be on board. It would make no sense for a company to shoot itself in the foot by placing an employee on a Decision Making Leave during annual inventory week, for example, when the presence of every team member is mandatory.

For these reasons, there will almost certainly be a time gap between the time the individual commits the disciplinary offense that provokes the decision to place her on a DML, and the time of the meeting at which she is told to leave and spend the following day at home making her decision. As a result, it's fairly easy to schedule the DML meeting at a time that's convenient for the company. It's also wise to schedule it at the end of the day. Having the person leave to begin the DML period at the end of her regular work day will not only be less disruptive, it will certainly be less embarrassing to the individual, who won't be forced to walk out in the middle of the work day.

Therefore, when a supervisor observes an employee committing a disciplinary violation that could result in the individual's being placed on a Decision Making Leave, the supervisor doesn't immediately place the employee on a DML. Instead, the supervisor says something like, "Jane, this is an extremely serious situation. I'm going to need to get all of the facts and make a decision about the best way to handle this. I'll get back with you to let you know when we will deal with it."

Having secured all necessary approvals and arranged the work schedule so that the employee's absence on DML will cause the minimum disruption possible, the manager can make the final arrangements for the meeting. Preparations will include reviewing the notes and documentation from the previous Reminder discussions, arranging for an appropriate location to hold the meeting, and arranging for any required witnesses or employee representative.

During the Meeting

The initial part of the meeting follows the same pattern as the earlier Reminder 1 and Reminder 2 discussions. The manager opens the meeting by describing specifically the issue that has caused the need for the discussion. He listens to what the employee has to say to confirm that there is no unknown reason for the Decision Making Leave transaction not to take place.

Having confirmed that a Decision Making Leave is appropriate, the manager explains the procedural elements of the Decision Making Leave in detail to make sure that there is no question or confusion on the employee's part.

The manager begins by telling the employee that following this meeting she is being placed on a Decision Making Leave, the final step of the company's disciplinary procedures. He advises the individual that immediately upon the conclusion of this meeting, she is to leave company premises for the rest of the day. She is told that she is being suspended from work on the following day and that she is to remain at home making a final decision about whether or not she can abide by company standards.

She is told that she must use this day to make a decision about her job once and for all: either to solve the immediate problem and make a total commitment to fully acceptable performance in every area of the job, or decide that working here is not for her and return with a decision to quit and find more satisfying employment somewhere else.

The employee should be advised that while the company will pay her for the day she is out, she must understand precisely what the company's expectations of her are and exactly where she stands. She is not simply to return to work on the day after her leave but must return with a final decision that she can live up to: either solve the problem once and for all and never create another situation that requires disciplinary action, or resign. She needs to be told that the reason the company is paying her is to indicate that the organization does hope that she will decide to change and stay, but that another problem that requires disciplinary action will result in her termination.

The employee should be advised exactly when she is due back (the beginning of her regularly scheduled work shift on the day following the Decision Making Leave) and what to do when she does return (come into the manager's office and advise her boss of the decision she has made.)

More than in any other disciplinary transaction, it is critical here that the employee confirm that she knows exactly what is expected and that there are no questions about exactly what she is to do.

Unlike previous conversations where the employee did most of the talking, now it is the manager who talks the most. The employee's responsibility is not so much to discuss the problem as it is to confirm her understanding of exactly what the company is instructing her to do. There is actually little real discussion that needs to take place at this point. Unless the situation represents such a grave violation that the company has moved directly to the Decision Making Leave, bypassing all initial steps, the problem has usually been talked to excess at this point. Over and over, the employee and manager have discussed the employee's failure to meet the company's standards, the employee has agreed to improve and meet at least the minimum standard of acceptable performance, and the employee has consistently failed to live up to her promise. The time for exploring various alternative approaches and training possibilities has passed.

The issue is now a straightforward matter of the employee's need to make a decision: Will she do what the company is paying her to do, or will she not? The company is now demanding, once and for all, that she make that a formal, conscious decision—one that she is prepared to live up to in the future, with expulsion from the organizational family the consequence if she fails. Other than clearly communicating that message, there is little else that needs to be said:

Manager: "Gerri, when we had both the Reminder 1 and Reminder 2 conversations, you agreed that you would solve this problem and perform your job in an acceptable manner. That hasn't happened. This morning the same problem came up again."

Employee: "Yeah, well, I tried, but sometimes things happen."

Manager: "Gerri, you really have to make a decision now about whether this really is the right job for you."

Employee: "Oh, yeah. Of course it is. I like working here."

Manager: "I'm glad to hear you say that, Gerri, but this problem keeps coming up. You really must make a serious decision about whether you can, in fact, solve this problem and meet all of the job requirements. That's why at the end of this meeting you will be placed on Decision Making Leave."

Employee: "You're gonna fire me?"

Manager: "No, Gerri. You're not being fired. You are being placed on Decision Making Leave, the final step of our discipline procedure. You are being suspended from work tomorrow. I want you to spend tomorrow thinking through whether this is the right job for you and whether you can solve this problem and perform every part of your job at a fully acceptable level."

Employee: "I don't need tomorrow off. I can tell you right now that I want my job."

Manager: "I want you to make that a real decision, Gerri. We are past the point of quick commitments that you don't live up to. That's why you will be out tomorrow. I want you to use your time tomorrow deciding either to solve this problem forever and make a commitment to fully acceptable performance in every area of your job, or decide to quit and get a job that's better for you."

Employee: "This job is fine with me. I can tell you right now what my decision will be."

Manager: "It isn't enough just to decide that you want to keep your job. Let me be real clear on exactly what you've got to do. Gerri, you can decide one of two things. You can decide that you will solve this problem and that you will also commit to doing your job so that there will never be any further problems—either this one or any other. Or you can decide to quit. Is the decision you've got to make clear?"

Employee: "Yeah. You want me to promise to do a good job."

Manager: "No, Gerri, that's not it. You've made us that promise before and you haven't lived up to it. Sorry, but that's the way it is. Now it requires more than that. When you come back the day after tomorrow I want you to come into my office and let me know what you have decided. It can be either to solve this problem plus agree to do every part of your job acceptably, or tell me that you're quitting. I can live with either choice, but you've got to make the decision."

Employee: "OK . . . I can shape up or ship out."

Manager: "That's right. I hope you do decide to change and stay with us. To indicate that we're serious about wanting to keep you on the team, you'll get full pay for the time you're out. We're not going to punish you or treat you like a little kid who's been naughty. You're an adult and you've got to accept adult responsibilities."

Employee: "So I'll get paid for tomorrow?"

Manager: "Yes. I don't want you to worry about your pay. I want you to concentrate on thinking about your job and whether you can do it right. Let me make sure you understand, Gerri. While I do hope that you decide to change and stay with us, if another problem comes up that requires disciplinary action, you can expect to be terminated."

Employee: "So if I do this again I'll get fired."

Manager: "Yes. But it's more than that. We are past the point of asking you just to solve this one problem. If you want to keep your job, Gerri, what you have to do is make a total commitment to good performance in every part of your job. That's because if another disciplinary problem comes up, this one or any other, I'll recommend that you be discharged."

Employee: "That's not fair!"

Manager: "What's not fair?"

Employee: "Expecting me agree to do every part of my job perfectly. I'm not perfect. Nobody's perfect. You're just setting a trap to fire me."

Manager: "I'm not asking you to be perfect. But I am telling you that we are at the last step of our discipline procedure, and if you want to keep your job you have to perform in a totally acceptable way. You must understand, Gerri, that if any other problem that requires disciplinary action arises, you can expect to be terminated. But I believe that if you think about it tomorrow, and decide to make a genuine change, you will be able to live up to it. You had

a solid record for several years before this problem got started . . .
I believe that you could get back to that if you tried.”

Employee: “Well, OK, but I really don’t need a day off.”

Manager: “It’s not an option, Gerri. We need for you to understand exactly how serious this situation really is. This is the final
step of the discipline procedure. You will be out tomorrow; you
must be back in here first thing Wednesday morning with your
final decision.”

Employee: “Ok. I’ll see you then.”

Manager: “Come on, I’ll walk out with you.”

Based on the manager’s experience with the individual and the
way the employee acts during the meeting, the manager may decide
to escort the person off the premises. As we see in the preceding case,
while the manager was communicating a friendly closure to the meeting, he was also making sure that the employee immediately left company premises and reduced the risks of any inappropriate behaviors
while the employee was leaving.

No formal documentation of the incident can take place until the
employee returns with her decision. It is important for the manager
to make some immediate notes about any important statements or
actions on the employee’s part during the meeting, but the manager’s
primary responsibility between the start and the completion of the
leave is to make sure that the employee’s work gets done.

When the Employee Returns

Most organizations that have implemented the Discipline Without
Punishment system report that the employee is usually waiting for the
manager on the morning following the Decision Making Leave day.
People do take it seriously. While cynics may scoff at giving people a
“vacation day,” and managers may be concerned about the appearance of rewarding bad behavior, almost universally the individuals
who receive a Decision Making Leave treat it very seriously indeed.

Not all of them live up to the commitments that they make, but few return with a casual response.

With surprising consistency managers report that people that they did not expect to respond as adults actually take personal responsibility for their own behavior when the chips are down. In the frequent number of cases where this does occur, managers also report that the relationship between themselves and the individual is strengthened. After the immediate emotional upheaval created by the Decision Making Leave has calmed and some time has passed, it is not uncommon for the employee to view the manager as that stern coach most of us admire; the one who held us to a high standard but expressed enough confidence in us that we stayed in the game when we were otherwise ready to quit.

Not everyone is transformed. Some come back with glowing words about how they have seen the light and will sin no more, but quickly return to their former ways and are terminated. Some return no more willing to take personal responsibility than they were when they left, seeing their problems as simply the result of fate or chance or a run of bad luck. They may perform badly enough to be discharged or just well enough to hang on, but never move up much from the bottom of the pile.

In a few cases, the employee votes with his feet and never shows up again.

In even fewer cases does the employee return and announce that he's resigning. The Decision Making Leave does cause many people to decide that it's time to change employers, but they see little payoff in precipitously resigning. They return, they perform sufficiently well to maintain membership in the family (and frequently they perform extremely well, concerned about the quality of reference they will receive), and within a few weeks or months find a new employer where they can get a fresh start. In almost every one of these cases, the decision turns out to be the best outcome for all.

But how do the results of the Decision Making Leave compare with the traditional unpaid disciplinary layoff as a final-step strategy? Without exception, managers report that the use of the Decision

Making Leave produces two significant advantages over the previous system:

1. More people actually do change, return to fully acceptable performance, and maintain that correction for a significant period of time.
2. The few people who continue to perform unacceptably following the DML are terminated with far less guilt and hesitation, and those terminations stick.

Managers who see the approach as soft when they first encounter it usually become advocates once they see the results. After the system had been in effect for a year, Tampa Electric surveyed exactly one hundred of their managers in the departments that were using it on a pilot basis. All but two agreed that the program should not only be continued but recommended its expansion. "When you get 98 out of 100 managers agreeing on anything," one senior executive observed, "you know you've got something that's very successful."

As soon as the employee arrives at work on the day following the leave, she should, as previously instructed, come into her boss's office and announce the decision she has made. This is a serious event and should be treated as such. There is only benefit to be gained by treating this occasion thoughtfully. Even a note of solemnity would not be out of place. Both the manager's words and demeanor should communicate that the organization considers this to be a recommitment to the standards that were accepted when the employee was first engaged. A cavalier, "Yeah, boss, I've thought it over and I've decided to stay," would be entirely inappropriate, and all of the manager's actions and behaviors should indicate that very serious business is at hand.

The supervisor may need to coach the employee to get the full commitment stated:

Manager: "I'm glad to see you, Gerri. What decision have you made?"

Employee: "Well, like I told you when I left, I really do want my job."

Manager: "And?"

Employee: "And I'm going to do it right."

Manager: And?

Employee: "Whattayamean, *and*? Isn't that enough?"

Manager: "Gerri, I was very clear with you before you left about exactly the decision you needed to make if you want to continue to work here. You have to decide not only that you want the job, but that you will solve the specific problem that we talked about and will do your job in a fully acceptable way."

Employee: "Well, sure, that's what I meant."

Manager: "So what is your decision?"

Employee: "Do I need to spell it out for you?"

Manager: "Yes, Gerri, you do. I need to know exactly what your decision is."

Employee: "Robert, I have decided that I do want to keep my job. I will solve the problem. I will do my job right. Is that OK?"

Manager: "Gerri, do you really mean it?"

Employee: "Yeah, Robert, I really do. I really did do a lot of thinking and I'm sorry about this whole thing. Like you said, we are never going to have to talk about this again."

At this point, the employee's decision is clear. The agreement has been reached. But this is the final step of the discipline procedure, and the employee also has the right to know what the failure to live up to her good intentions will involve:

Manager: "Gerri, I'm glad that you made that choice. I was hoping that you would because you're a valuable part of this team and I don't want to lose you."

Employee: "Thanks."

Manager: "But you do need to know where you stand. This is the last step of the company's Discipline Without Punishment system. There aren't any more chances after this. If another problem comes up—this one or anything else, whatever it may be—that requires disciplinary action, you can expect that you will be terminated. I don't want that to happen, you don't want that to happen, and I need your commitment that it's never gonna happen."

Employee: "Robert, you've got it. Believe me, we are never going to talk about this or anything like it again."

The employee has now been advised of the future consequences if this or any other problem arises. It is now time for the manager to wrap things up:

Manager: "Gerri, I'm glad you have made this decision, and quite honestly I believe that we will never have to talk about it again. Since this is the final step of our discipline procedure, as soon as this meeting is over I will be writing you a memo confirming our conversation and your agreement to solve this problem and perform acceptably in every area of your job. In that memo, Gerri, I will also be advising you again of what I just said—that if any further problems come up that require disciplinary action, the logical consequence is termination."

Employee: "Don't rub it in."

Manager: "That's not my intent. But I do need to make it real clear."

Employee: "It's clear."

Manager: "You also know that this is active for eighteen months. You live up to your commitment, this comes out of your file."

Employee: "I can do that."

Manager: "I know you can, Gerri. Now let's get back to work and put this behind us."

With that, the employee leaves. The only things left for the manager to do are to document the Decision Making Leave transaction and then to monitor the employee's performance to make sure that the problem once solved, stays solved.

Documenting the Decision Making Leave

The documentation requirements for the Decision Making Leave are virtually the same as those for the Reminder 2. The specific details of the problem need to be recorded as well as the complete history of any earlier discussions about the situation and, most important, a record of the exact agreement the employee made and a statement of the consequences to follow if the agreement is not maintained.

After the memo has been prepared, it should be reviewed in a brief meeting with the employee. The individual should be asked to confirm that the memo reasonably reflects the content of the discussions between herself and the manager and, more important, the agreement that the employee made as a result of the Decision Making Leave. The manager's positive expectation of change and correction should also be communicated, as well as a final restatement of the fact that any further problems will logically result in termination.

Should the employee be required to sign the memo to acknowledge receipt? While the chances that the signature will ever be useful are slight, there may, at this final step, be more value in requesting the signature than there was at the Reminder 2 stage.

At the time of the Reminder 2, the organization still had the Decision Making Leave in its arsenal if the employee did not live up to the agreement he had made. At the point of Decision Making Leave, there is no further disciplinary step available. If the employee fails to perform acceptably, he will be terminated. There may be value in emphasizing the importance of the commitment by asking for a signature, not merely to acknowledge receipt of the memo, but to affirm positively the commitment to perform acceptably in the future.

Appendix D is an example of a memo documenting a Decision Making Leave transaction.

If Further Problems Arise

When the employee returns from Decision Making Leave it is critical that he be advised that this is the final step of the company's discipline procedure and that any further problems, of any kind, will be met by termination. Whether you actually will terminate the individual if another problem comes up will depend on several factors, including how long it has been since the Decision Making Leave took place, the specific violation that occurred, how the employee's overall performance has been, what you have done with other people who have committed similar infractions, and the like.

It is important that the integrity of the system be maintained. If employees discover that management ignores problems following a Decision Making Leave, the overall performance of the organization is likely to decline. Highly motivated and committed performers become discouraged when they discover that the organization condones irresponsibility on the part of both the leaders and the led. Sluggards and organizational ne'er-do-wells will revel in this laissez-faire atmosphere where little is demanded and less is produced.

When problems arise after a Decision Making Leave, our human compassion may tempt us to give the employee a second chance. But is it a "second chance" we are actually providing? Most people in any company never create disciplinary problems. The few who do, usually clean up their act after a Reminder 1. The few who do not, usually shape up after a Reminder 2. The few who still do not, usually come to their when senses they preview unemployment on a Decision Making Leave. So the tiny few who do not perform at the minimum level tolerable following the Decision Making Leave step are not really asking for a second chance. Having had a second chance, and a third, and a fourth, they plead for a fifth. In the absence of gravely mitigating circumstances it is time to say, "Enough's enough," cut your losses, and hire a replacement who will appreciate employment with your organization.

It is a particularly bad idea, if the employee continues to create problems after a Decision Making Leave, to try a more traditional step like an unpaid layoff of several days instead of terminating the individual. First, moving to a punitive response will damage the integrity of the system. It will communicate to all that management only talks about dealing with employees as mature and responsible adults, but when push comes to shove, they still deal with them as children.

Second, it increases the probability that employees who are finally terminated from the organization will be returned if they appeal their discharge. The arbitrator or hearing officer, seeing that the organization's actual discipline policy (as opposed to the one officially stated in the policy manual) provides for an unpaid layoff of perhaps three days after he had received a Decision Making Leave, might order the employee reinstated but with an unpaid layoff of five days this time. But if the organization can demonstrate that it consistently has given people a fair chance to get problems solved through a series of increasingly progressive but nonpunitive steps and then terminates anyone who fails to perform acceptably after the final step, the chances that an outside third party would force the company to take the employee back are much smaller.

Common Questions About the Decision Making Leave

Question: *What if the employee is late getting back from DML or calls in asking for more time?*

Answer: If the employee calls in asking for more time, refuse the request and demand that he return immediately at the beginning of his next scheduled work shift with his answer.

If the employee is late, ask why. Unless there are powerfully mitigating circumstances, the wisest course would be to terminate the person for failure to return from leave as scheduled.

If an individual calls in "sick" or presents some other excuse for failure to return as scheduled, termination is probably the appropriate course.

In each of these cases we are not dealing with the average employee of the organization. We are not even dealing with the average problem employee. We are dealing with the problem employee who has completely lost control of his ability to act rationally and in his own obvious best interests. He is standing on the precipice of termination waiting to see if we will rush to his rescue and pull him back from the abyss.

Do not rush. Let him fall.

Question: *Are there any employees for whom a Decision Making Leave is not appropriate?*
Answer: The only employees for whom a Decision Making Leave would not be appropriate would be those whose commitment to the enterprise is unimportant. It might, perhaps, be unnecessary to give a Decision Making Leave to a seasonal worker when most of the season's work is complete. But in any organization where a continuing high standard of performance and a high degree of organizational commitment is important, the Decision Making Leave is appropriate.

One big advantage of the Decision Making Leave is that it can be used at higher organizational levels where conventional disciplinary steps often seem inappropriate. It would be awkward to tell a vice president that he was being placed on probation or to give a senior scientist a three-day unpaid suspension. But problems of attendance, performance, and conduct aren't restricted to the factory floor. Both of these individuals could be given a Decision Making Leave with powerful effect. Since both are exempt employees, the issue of pay for the day is irrelevant, but the effect of being refused admission to the premises for one day and compelled to reconsider one's commitment to the enterprise would be both dignified and powerful.

Question: *What if the employee refuses to make any decision at all?*
Answer: This question invariably comes up when I explain the approach to managers during executive overviews of Discipline Without Punishment. "What do we do," someone will ask, "if the guy just stands there when he comes back and says that he's not going to quit and he's not going to make any agreements?"

In this case we are dealing with a disturbed individual. It is extremely rare for someone to return from a Decision Making Leave and refuse to agree.

Let's be clear about what it is that the company is asking the employee to agree to do. We are not asking him to perform at a superior level or even at a mediocre level. All that we are asking is that he agree not to create any problems which will provoke his termination; to perform at any level above that of unacceptability. Our demands of him could not be lower. If he is unable or unwilling to agree to solve a problem that has caused him to arrive at the company's final disciplinary step, and refuses further to agree to perform his job at the minimum level of acceptability, we do not need his services. The best approach would be to tell him bluntly that his response is unacceptable, that he must either decide to correct the problem or announce that he is quitting, and the company will consider his failure to respond appropriately to be an act of insubordination for which termination is the proper remedy. Unless an immediate response of commitment to acceptable performance is received, suspend the person pending investigation and then terminate for insubordination.

Question: *What if the employee never returns from the DML?*
Answer: First, make an immediate attempt to determine whether he has involuntarily been prevented from returning by an accident or emergency. Almost all individuals return promptly following a Decision Making Leave. Supervisors regularly report that they find the individual there waiting for them when they arrive on the morning they are due back.

If the individual simply does not return, most organizations provide that three days of "no-call, no-show" constitutes job abandonment and terminate the individual for that reason.

Question: *What if the person comes back while he's supposed to be on Decision Making Leave and starts to work?*
Answer: This happens more than you would think.

The fact that employees frequently show up for work when they are supposed to be away on Decision Making Leave strongly refutes the misconception that they will not take the step seriously but will intentionally misbehave in order to "get another vacation day."

As soon as the manager sees the employee, he should tell him to stop working and direct him to come into the manager's office or some other private area. Ask the employee what he is doing. In most cases, the individual is so embarrassed by having been placed on the Decision Making Leave that he is dealing with his feelings through denial. While we may sympathize, it is not a matter of the individual's choice. Tell him that this is a formal disciplinary step and that he is to leave immediately and return on the following day with his decision.

Unless there was any more to the incident than a misunderstanding or the individual's attempt to deny the reality of the step, do not make any further reference to the event and let it go as a misunderstanding.

Question: *What do I say if other employees ask, "Where's Harry?"*
Answer: Say, "Harry's out today." If they continue to ask, tell them that that is Harry's business and that just as you would honor and respect their privacy, so you honor and respect his.

Question: *What do I do if the employee says he can decide during the Decision Making Leave meeting? Can I accept his decision on the spot?*
Answer: No. Employees frequently offer a decision immediately upon being advised of the Decision Making Leave in order to avoid the shame of having to spend the day away from work (again rebutting the notion that the Decision Making Leave rewards bad behavior). He sounds so contrite and sincere that it's is tempting to accept the employee's decision on the spot and process the paperwork as though the DML had actually occurred or to reflect that the employee's decision was accepted in lieu of his spending the day away from work on the DML. This is invariably a bad idea.

As sincere as the individual may sound, this will turn out to be the case where the employee will continue his mischief and receive a well-earned discharge. But when he challenges the termination, as invariably these types do, his defense will be that the company did not follow its own policies in terminating him. The Decision Making Leave is not an option.

Question: *Is it fair to ask for a "total performance commitment"?*
Answer: The most meaningful difference between the Decision Mak-

ing Leave and the traditional unpaid disciplinary suspension is not that the employee is paid for the period he is away from work while on a DML. That is the most obvious difference, but not the most important.

The most important difference between the two final-step strategies lies in what the organization asks of the individual who reaches this point. The traditional approach asks nothing more of the employee than that he serve out his time. When the unpaid suspension period has been completed, the employee typically returns to his workplace and picks up his hammer where he had put it down. He may be reprimanded for what he has done, he may warned that if he does it again he will be fired, but he is not required to make any affirmative commitment to the organization or any positive resolution regarding his future behavior.

The Decision Making Leave rejects the traditional approach, not only because it is punitive but because it is insufficiently demanding. Now the employee must do more than amuse himself for the three days that he is off the payroll. Now he must stand before his boss and announce his decision, with whatever level of sincerity he can muster, about his future as a member of the organizational family. And the commitment he is being asked for is not merely a commitment to solve the immediate problem that triggered the Decision Making Leave, but the commitment to totally acceptable performance in every area of his job.

CHAPTER 8

Discharge

Most people who are placed on a Decision Making Leave return with a decision to change. Most live up to that commitment. They correct the problem and maintain fully acceptable performance.

A few people fail to make the changes required to maintain membership in the organization. In these cases, termination is appropriate.

Finally, situations do arise where firing an individual is the right thing to do, even though no steps of disciplinary action have previously been taken.

Is Discharge Punitive?

A frequent misunderstanding involves the belief that while the Discipline Without Punishment system seems to have abolished minor forms of punishment (warnings, reprimands, unpaid suspensions), it retains the most severe form of punishment—termination.

This misunderstanding results from the traditional progressive-discipline system's notion that termination is the final step of the discipline system: verbal reprimand, written warning, suspension without pay, discharge. But discharge is not the final step of the discipline system. Discharge represents the failure of the discipline system.

Consider this: The purpose of any discipline system, whether a traditional progressive-discipline approach or a nonpunitive procedure, is to convince the individual to stop his unacceptable behaviors and return to a fully acceptable level of performance. When a person returns from Decision Making Leave and continues to perform at an unacceptable level, there is no evidence that there's any further action we can take that will bring him to his senses and convince him to fly right. At this point we decide to terminate his employment. Everything we have done to convince the individual to take responsibility for his behavior, correct that behavior, and return to acceptable norms has failed. He must find employment with another employer who is willing to accept him; we must find a replacement who will meet our standards.

Even when we terminate for a first offense, the purpose is not punishment. In these cases, usually involving major offenses like theft or assault or some other outrageous behavior, we terminate the individual not to punish the offender but because by committing that one intolerable act he has forfeited the right to the benefit of corrective action. By committing an act of theft, or assaulting a fellow employee, or selling drugs on the premises, he has demonstrated so little self-esteem and ability to conform to the minimum demands of a civilized society that his presence can no longer be tolerated.

Years ago I heard a labor relations attorney make the statement, "Discharge is the capital punishment of organizational life." Capital punishment! If that's the metaphor we have for termination, no wonder organizations and their managers are so hesitant to fire a nonperforming member of the team.

"Capital punishment" is absolutely the wrong way to think about termination. What's the appropriate metaphor? A no-fault divorce. When an organization that uses Discipline Without Punishment reaches the point of discharge, in effect the organization is saying to the employee: "You're a good person. We're a good company. But your needs and style, and our needs and style, are incompatible. We've tried several times to bridge the gap, but those efforts have failed. You need to find an employer who's right for you; we need to find someone else who's right for us." As painful as divorce may be at the time, it allows two people to correct a mistake and move on to a more satisfying future. That's the objective of discharge in Discipline Without Punishment.

Reaching the Termination Decision

The easiest firings are those produced by unexpected crises. Unprovoked, one employee hauls off and belts another. Your purchasing agent is revealed to be taking money on the sly. Two young summer interns are discovered, *in flagrante*, on the boardroom table.

These are easy. The provocation is clear and the remedy is obvious.

But these easy cases are rare. More difficult are those situations where the employee returns from a Decision Making Leave and subsequently commits an offense that would provoke a Performance Improvement Discussion or a Reminder 1 if it had been committed by an employee with an unblemished record. That's why it's important for the memo documenting the Decision Making Leave to contain a statement that informs the employee that he must maintain a completely satisfactory record in all parts of his job. A statement like this will make the point clear: "As I advised you during our meeting, you must immediately correct this situation. In addition, you must maintain fully acceptable performance in every area of your job, since any further problems that require disciplinary action, whether related to this issue or not, will result in your termination."

The most difficult terminations arise with an individual who receives a Decision Making Leave because her performance is simply not up to par. After her return she struggles to do the job right, but in spite of her sincere efforts her performance still is unacceptable and no compatible job exists within the organization.

Whatever scenario produces the decision to terminate, the manager's first responsibility is to the enterprise itself. Arrange the termination so that it occurs with the least damage to the company and fellow workers.

Creating a Plan

Start by creating a transition plan.

Good plans have three parts. The first part covers all the things you need to do before meeting with the individual to announce the termination. The second part involves the actual face-to-face meeting with the terminatee. This is your script—the exact words you will say to open the meeting and the checklist of points you will cover while the two of you are together. The final part of your plan covers exactly what will happen once the two of you shake hands and part company forever.

Virtually no organization allows managers to make a termination decision unilaterally. In every case the decision to end someone's employment needs to be weighed and approved by senior officers in the line organization and the personnel function. Often the president or company owner is involved.

Getting a couple of senior managers to review the plan to terminate an individual will greatly increase the odds that wise decisions will be made. In addition, if the termination is ever challenged later, the fact that the decision to terminate was made only after several senior individuals in the organization reviewed and approved the termination greatly adds to the defensibility of the action.

In creating the transition plan, choose the day and the time for the termination deliberately. While experts disagree on when a firing should occur, all acknowledge the importance of having a rationale—a good business reason for your choice of time and day for dropping the ax. Doing it early in the day, early in the week, encourages the employee to get right to work on finding another job and reduces the chances that he'll spend the weekend moping in a black hole or, worse, plotting revenge. Friday afternoons, on the other hand, often create the minimum amount of disruption to the rest of the staff.

Whatever your decision, put company interests first. For months you have probably put up with less than stellar performance in hopes that the situation would somehow correct itself. Now that the end is at hand, plan the transition to do the least damage to company and coworkers. You may want to start recruiting and wait to terminate until you've got a replacement ready to go. It may be in your best interests to send some subtle signals to clients and customers that there will be a staffing change soon.

If security is an issue, be prepared to escort the employee off the premises as soon as the termination has been announced. In industries like banking or computer software, where sabotage is a risk, restricting entry may be an unpleasant but necessary precaution. Every manager has heard horror stories of employees who left behind chaos by spitting gum in the works on their way out.

In addition, consider having another person present when you make the announcement that the individual has been terminated. Having another member of management in the room is particularly important if you are concerned about the possibility of violence or other inappropriate behavior, or in those cases where the termination meeting involves a male supervisor and a female employee.

Run It By a Jury First

A good way to make sure that you are on solid ground in terminating an employee is to imagine yourself defending your action in front of a jury. Assume that you are on the witness stand and the employee's lawyer is attempting to prove that the firing was unjust, unfair, and vindictive.

Consider the questions the lawyer is likely to ask. The appropriate use of the Discipline Without Punishment system will convincingly answer all of the standard questions raised by a plaintiff's attorney:

• Was the employee fully aware that his performance was unacceptable?

- How do you know that he knew?
- How often did you talk about it?
- Have there been any disciplinary discussions?
- Do you have any documentation?
- Was he given time to improve?
- Was adequate training provided?
- Can you prove it?
- Is there any information in the original employment application and other hiring data to suggest that poor placement is the real problem?

Look for anything that could be twisted to suggest that the real reason for the termination is not the individual's performance but rather a personal grudge. Isn't that the real reason why you fired poor Smedley on his birthday, on the day before his tenth anniversary with the company, on the day before his pension vested, on the day his wife went into the hospital, on the day before his vacation started, on the day his mom died?

Don't fail to check any performance evaluations. Is there a record of unacceptable appraisals that confirm the disciplinary transactions? What do the last three evaluations actually say? Many times managers sugarcoat their appraisal ratings to avoid a confrontation, only to discover later on that the employee whose employment they want to terminate appears to be a model worker who possesses no significant flaws. This possibility is a particularly important reason for demanding that performance appraisals be written honestly and that the truth be told, even when the truth isn't pleasant. It's a wise policy to require that all performance evaluations be reviewed and approved by the appraiser's immediate supervisor before they are discussed with the employee. In this way, senior managers can make sure that known poor performers do not receive inflated performance appraisals. HR specialists should also check to make sure that appraisals of employees who are on active steps of disciplinary action reflect honestly the fact that there were serious problems during the appraisal period.

Finally, are there any mitigating circumstances? Could a jury of his peers, neutral and unbiased, come to the conclusion that you acted outrageously?

In spite of all the publicity regarding wrongful termination cases, few employees ever take their former boss to court. The best way to keep out of court is to put yourself in the shoes of an arbitrator, a plaintiff's attorney, an EEOC investigator, or some other skeptical third party. Ask yourself how you would go about arguing that the employee was fired for some reason other than poor performance, unacceptable attendance, or inappropriate conduct. Then eliminate those reasons.

It may be that a careful review of the facts indicates that there are mitigating circumstances important enough that you decide not to proceed with termination in a case that initially appeared to justify the employee's discharge. In this case, it's critical that the reasons for the decision not to terminate be documented. There may be good reasons for making an exception in George's case and to decide not to terminate him for a problem that would have resulted in termination had it arisen with someone else. But be sure to make a complete record of exactly why the decision was made not to terminate so that you can demonstrate a reasonable consistency in the future. It may also be appropriate to write George a memo, reviewing the facts of the case and indicating that while terminating him was considered, the company decided not to do so for whatever the reasons may have been. Having this memo on file may be beneficial if you later discharge another person in a similar situation who claims that exceptions were made in the past. Yes, they were, your records will indicate, but there were good reasons in that case that are not present in this one.

Finally, consider providing the employee with some form of appeal procedure. No matter how valid the termination may be, many employees want a chance to have their side of the story heard. Providing for arbitration is one possibility. A "peer review" procedure, where a panel of managers and nonmanagement coworkers is empowered to hear employee grievances and make final and binding decisions to uphold or reverse terminations, demonstrates management's commitment to making the right decision. Even allowing for a formal appeal to the president or chief HR officer may provide the employee with the feeling that he's had his day in court. While providing any kind of appeal mechanism may seem cumbersome and unnecessary, if there is no internal way for an employee to challenge what he feels is a bum decision, his only recourse is lawyers, government agencies, and the courts.

Preparing a Script

Bungled terminations usually result from the manager's acting without thinking. Before you utter a word, write down the most important things you plan to say and then stick to your script.

Start by recognizing what you're up to. This is not a counseling session or a discussion about poor performance or another Discipline Without Punishment step. It is the announcement of an irrevocable decision to discharge the individual.

1. Get right to the point. Skip the small talk. Don't put off the inevitable. All of your attempts to "put the person at ease" will backfire if you don't get immediately to the job at hand. Start by saying, "Hello, John. Thank you for coming in. I've got some bad news for you." By announcing right from the start that there is bad news ahead, you will rivet the individual's attention on what's coming next.

2. Break the bad news. State the reason for the termination in one or two short sentences and then tell the person directly that he has been terminated: "As you know, John, we have talked several times about quality problems in your area. You have been through all the steps of our Discipline Without Punishment procedure. But last month's report indicated that your unit still has the lowest quality index. We have decided that a change must be made, and as of today your employment has been terminated."

Or, "Sally, we've talked before about your failure to respond promptly to customer inquiries and complaints. When you returned from your Decision Making Leave you told me that you would correct the problem completely, but since then I have had two more complaints from customers. After these last complaints I realized that the situation is not working out. I have decided that a change must be made and that today will be your last day with us."

Or, "Walt, when your forklift hit the wall yesterday, I told you that this was a very serious safety problem. I said then that I would need to get all of the information and get back to you to let you know what we would do. I have now completed my investigation of the accident. Because of the seriousness of this incident, we have decided to terminate your employment with the company."

In each case, the manager is focusing on the problem or the performance, not on the person. There is no need to be brutal. John or Sally or Walt is still an honorable and worthwhile human being. He or she is simply no longer an employee of your company.

In the course of writing down exactly what you will say to break the bad news, ask yourself the question, "What do I know for sure?" The answer to that question will help you decide how to phrase your announcement. For example, you don't know for sure that John is unconcerned with quality. You do know that he is the section supervisor and that his section has the lowest quality index of any. You don't know for sure that Sally doesn't care about handling customer complaints quickly. You do know that you recently received two more letters from customers objecting to the way their complaints were handled. And you don't know for sure that Walt is a reckless driver; you do know that he ran his forklift into the wall.

Note that in each of these cases, the manager directly announces that the employee has been terminated. The individual is being told of something that has already happened, not advised of something that will happen in the future. It is easier to focus the individual's attention on the fact that his future lies elsewhere if he clearly hears the statement that the decision has been made, the door has been shut. The decision cannot be revoked or reversed. The ball game is over.

3. Listen to what the employee has to say. There are several predictable reactions to the news that one has just lost her job. The most common are shock, denial, anger, and grief. Listening to what the employee says will tell you which of the reactions she is experiencing.

Your response will be more effective if you know how she is taking the news.

Listening carefully will also tell you whether she has accepted the reality that she is no longer a member of the organization. You can't move forward to talk about what will happen from here on until she accepts the fact her employment is through.

Listening also demonstrates compassion. When people complain to the EEOC, a state human rights commission, or other third party, their initial complaint frequently involves not their belief that they were discriminated against but their feeling that they weren't treated fairly. Treating someone unfairly, while deplorable, is usually not illegal. Treating someone fairly—giving her a chance to explain; listening to what he has to say—can often eliminate the individual's desire to complain about mistreatment to an outsider.

When you listen to the now-former employee's response to the news that she has been discharged, avoid the tendency to be a counselor. Don't argue about whether a good decision has been made. For better or worse, the die has been cast and it is in the best interest of both parties to move on to brighter tomorrows.

How is the employee taking the news? If the reaction is *shock*, don't try to prove to the person that she should have seen it coming. Instead, acknowledge the emotion and make sure that the message gets across.

Anger is the reaction that managers fear the most: "You can't do this to me! I'll show you! I'll get you for this!" We've been spooked by so many, "Unhappy Worker Guns Down Boss," headlines that we anticipate its possibility any time we lower the boom. Fortunately, anger is the least common response. Anger can be diffused by listening and avoiding any debate about the merits of the action. Be firm, repeat the decision, and let the employee vent his feelings. Then say, "I can see that you're angry, Paul. It's an understandable reaction. What you need to do, though, is channel your energy into thinking about what you're going to do next."

Denial may be the most difficult reaction to deal with. There have been several cases where an employee who had been told that he had been fired went right back to his desk and picked up where he had left off before the meeting, explaining that there were several projects he had to finish before he could leave. When, "I can't believe that this is happening," is the response, your job is to make sure the employee gets the message. Repeat, restate, and talk about what the next steps will be.

Grief is almost always present, and no manager should begin a termination discussion without a box of tissues at arm's reach. When the need arises, take the box, offer a tissue, wait until the employee has regained his composure somewhat, and keep the discussion moving.

Whatever the reaction, listening to the employee will increase the odds that the person will accept the unhappy decision maturely and concentrate his attention on moving to the next stage of his career. Nodding silently while the employee is speaking, making the sounds that indicate that you're paying attention ("Auh-huh," "I see," "um-mmmm," etc.), and pausing after you ask a question will demonstrate that you've heard the person out.

Keep It Short

Once you have written your script for the meeting, it is wise to prepare a written termination summary that spells out all of the information the person needs to know. The termination summary will answer questions like these:

- How long will I continue to be paid?
- What will happen to my health insurance? My life insurance? My retirement plan, or 401(k)?
- What support can I expect in looking for a new job? Access to an office? A phone? Outplacement assistance?
- What will be said when people call about a reference?

Putting a written termination statement in the individual's hand helps the manager communicate that the decision is irrevocable. It also demonstrates the organization's belief that the interests of both parties are best served if there is a clear statement that summarizes all of the issues that surround the termination. Finally, the termination statement helps keep the meeting short.

At this point there's not much to talk about. The time for coaching and problem solving has passed. Once the employee has accepted the reality of the termination, reviewing the details of the termination statement is the first step toward beginning a new life in a different place.

If the person still hasn't fully accepted the finality of the situation, explain how you will present the termination to people inside the company and then ask, "How do you plan to break the news to your family and friends?"

Bring the meeting to a close by specifically explaining the next step. When the employee asks, "What do I do now?" you should be able to answer that question in detail. If you are fortunate enough to have the services of an outplacement counselor, the answer is to take the person to the room where the counselor is waiting, introduce the two of them, and let the professional take over. If you're doing it on your own, decide whether the employee can go back to her work area or must exit company premises immediately. If she can return to the work area, will it be to finish the rest of the day or just to clear personal belongings out her desk? If she is leaving directly, how will she get her stuff?

If you're doing it without outside help, it's usually best to schedule the termination meeting at the end of a work day so that the meeting takes place while coworkers are leaving. After the meeting (ten minutes is sufficient, more than twenty is excessive) walk with the employee back to his desk and wait while he collects any personal items. Anything too big can be put in one corner for later pickup or delivery; the rest can be taken directly. Walk to the exit together, shake hands, wish him well, and part with both of your dignities intact.

Avoiding Misdirected Compassion

One final note. Thirty-five years of watching the management scene has convinced me that the biggest problem with terminations is that they don't happen often enough.

Most managers are compassionate people, but when the need arises to terminate a subordinate their compassion is often misdirected. They become so concerned about the adverse impact on the employee to be discharged that they forget about all the people who manage to do their jobs and meet our expectations in spite of having as many personal problems and difficulties as the terminatee has.

Managers are also concerned about the risks involved in terminating someone, particularly when that person is a member of a minority group or some other protected class. But there are also great risks in not terminating someone whose performance and behavior are not acceptable. Bad apples do infect good ones. They are more likely to be union sympathizers or organizers. We do a disservice to our clients and customers by allowing marginal employees to remain on the payroll. And companies can face claims of negligent retention when a troubled individual is allowed to remain after evidence of problems has become apparent.

The issue is not one of risk avoidance. It is one of risk selection. And when the processes I've outlined in this chapter have been followed, the risks of not terminating will almost always be greater than the risks that accompany the choice to retain a poor performer.

While managers are appropriately concerned with how one person's termination will affect the rest of the work group, usually they discover that coworkers are actually relieved. His peers are the ones who have had to work harder to make up for his shortcomings and sloughings off. When terminations are well justified and professionally executed, the rest of the work group realizes that the discipline system actually works. If the termination is handled with dignity and grace, the notion that this is a good place to work is strengthened.

But when obvious losers and shirkers and occupational ne'er-do-wells are allowed to continue in their positions unchallenged, the message to the talented and energetic is that this is a place to avoid. Those who can find other jobs leave; the ones who stay are those who prefer an employer with low standards.

CHAPTER 9

Solving Attendance and Attitude Problems

Of all of the problems that supervisors in organizations have to deal with, the two that are most commonly reported are those of attitude and absenteeism. In this chapter we explore successful ways to deal with each of these common problems.

Attendance

It's probably not the world's most pressing problem, but you wouldn't know it from talking to supervisors. Ask any bunch of managers what their most difficult challenge is and they'll all tell you the same thing: How go I get people to come to work? Here's how to solve the vexing problem of attendance control.

Cause Is Irrelevant

First and most important, memorize these words: The *cause* of any absence is irrelevant. Only the *effect* counts.

Consider two employees, each of whom is absent from work on a given Tuesday. The first was out because she ate at a low-rent restaurant Monday night, picked up a dose of food poisoning, and was utterly incapable of coming to work the following day. (By the way, doctors will tell you that about the only medical condition that so debilitates people that they are incapable of working on one day, with a recovery period so swift that they can show up for work on the next day, is food poisoning. The 24-hour flu is a myth.) The second employee left for work on that Tuesday morning, noticed that it was a beautiful day, and said, "Blow it off. I'm calling in sick and going fishing!"

Here's the question: In which case did the job get done better?

Wait a minute! That's not the question you were expecting. But it's the right question to ask. Regardless of the quality of the excuse, the fact remains—if the employee doesn't come to work, the job doesn't get done, and it ultimately makes no difference why the employee is absent.

That's the hardest message to communicate about attendance. Whatever the reason for the absence, the effect is always the same: The job doesn't get done. Good reason, poor reason, no reason—it makes no difference. Your customers don't care why your staff is missing. They just know that they aren't being served.

But presented with an absence, supervisors invariably make things worse by carelessly asking, "Why were you out?" The only response that badly chosen question provokes is an airy excuse, offered up with all the sincerity the employee can muster. The supervisor's typical rejoinder: "That's not a very good excuse!" So what does the message to Molly Malingerer become? Come up with a better excuse.

What Do You Know for Sure?

There is a better way. First, ask yourself the critical question, what do I know *for sure*? Simply put, you never know for sure whether the employee was sick or had car troubles or was the victim of an irresponsible child-care provider. What you do know for sure is that when the doors opened for business, the employee wasn't there.

Next, explain to employees that the organization's attendance policy is simple and clear: This company expects the staff to show up, fully prepared, on time, every day, clean, straight, and sober, for the entire duration of the work day. Any variation from that is a failure to meet expectations and a violation of policy.

"But I've got sick leave!" some employees will complain. And so the second common misunderstanding about attendance presents itself.

There is no way in which companies more consistently shoot themselves in the foot than in their administration of an odious little policy called, *sick leave*.

The "Sick Leave" Misunderstanding

Where in your company's big policy binder is your "sick leave" policy housed? In too many organizations, it's stuck in with the procedures regarding absences from work, like vacations and jury duty and holidays and bereavement leaves.

Take it out of there! Filing it there is what causes so much employee misunderstanding. Sick leave has nothing to do with time off from work. But we continually and erroneously send our employees that message. Your sick leave plan needs to be filed with your policies that deal with money, like tuition refund, health insurance, and accidental death and dismemberment insurance.

Sick leave has nothing to do with holidays or vacations or bereavement leaves or other forms of time off from work. Sick leave is essentially an *insurance policy*, just like life insurance or collision coverage on your car. Just because we give you life insurance doesn't mean we want you to die; just because you have collision coverage doesn't mean you should drive your car into a tree. Just because we'll refund your tuition if you successfully compete certain courses doesn't mean you can leave the job to attend them. And just because you have sick leave doesn't mean we want you to take time off from work.

The purpose of "sick leave" is to provide income protection for a certain number of days when you are unable to work for a specifically defined set of reasons. But it has nothing to do with your attendance expectation. Courts and arbitrators have consistently upheld the right of an organization to terminate people for failure to maintain regular attendance even when all of the absences have been for legitimate medical necessity, each has been confirmed by medical certification, and the employee has sick leave in the bank.

So clean up your language. Abolish the inappropriate phrase, *sick leave*, and replace it with an accurate one: our *income protection policy*. After years of being misinformed, employees need to be reeducated about the purpose and intent of the policy formerly known as sick leave.

Never Call It "Excessive Absenteeism"

Another language bugaboo arises with the phrase supervisors incessantly use to label the concern they have with an employee's failure to show up at work: "excessive absenteeism." Think about it: If the employee's absenteeism is *excessive*, then there must be some *acceptable* amount of absenteeism that the employee has exceeded.

Never use the phrase "excessive absences" as a reason for disciplinary action or termination. Using this phrase suggests that there is some standard of acceptability that the individual has exceeded. If you are challenged, the first question you'll be asked is, What's the standard? Don't allow yourself to get caught in that trap.

Instead, use the appropriate phrase: "Failure to maintain regular attendance." What is "regular attendance"? It is: showing up, fully prepared, on time, every day, clean, straight, and sober, for the entire duration of the shift.

The Truth About Doctor's Certificates

Even worse than confusing employees with a misnamed sick leave policy, the organization further compounds its problems by asking malingerers and goldbricks to bring in a doctor's certificate when they've stayed away from work for a while. What's the purpose of a doctor's certificate? There are three.

One reason companies ask for medical certification is to make sure that the employee who has suffered a contagious or communicable disease is no longer in an infectious state upon returning to work.

That's probably the real reason for asking for a doctor's statement in perhaps one-half of 1 percent of all cases.

The second reason we ask for a note from the doctor is to assure ourselves that the employee who has suffered an illness or injury is, in fact, able to return to work without putting her own health at risk. And that's likely to be the reason for asking for a physician's release in another one-half of 1 percent of all cases.

In the other 99 percent of all cases, the reason for asking for a doctor's certificate is harassment. Our theory is that if we force them to spend their time and money to visit Doc Sawbones to pick up a note, they'll be more likely to figure it's easier just to come into work.

A better approach is to create your own doctor's certificates. Instead of asking the individual to bring you a doctor's certificate after she's played hooky for a while, give her one of yours. Just prepare a little form for a doctor to fill out that reads something like this:

This is to certify that _____ (name of employee) was under my care and unable to work on _____ (dates) because of _____ (medical condition).

I understand that this certification may be use in a court of law, arbitration, or other proceeding in the event that the individual is terminated for failure to maintain regular attendance.

Signed: _____, M.D.

Under what conditions will a doctor sign a notice like that? Of course—when the employee's health condition necessitates absence from work.

Building Personal Responsibility

But all of this discussion still skirts the real issue: How do we build individual responsibility in each employee so that he understands that coming to work is, in fact, a condition of employment?

It starts by having supervisors shuck off excuses and focus instead on delivering the personal-responsibility message. In counseling an employee about the need to be at work on time every day, it's important for the supervisor to start by stressing the organization's attendance expectation. The statement that the supervisor then should be making to the employee is, "Sally, I understand that you may have (child care problems / medical difficulties / car troubles / runaway pets / etc.). The fact is, we need someone who can show up for work every day. If you can't come to work every day that you're scheduled, I will need to find someone who can. Now what are you going to do so that you can meet your responsibility for showing up on time every day?"

"I'll try to improve," is the least acceptable answer an absentee can offer up. There's no genuine agreement here. All the individual has proposed is a promise to try. When the next day of absence arises, the rejoinder, "Well, I tried," will invariably be extended.

Trying doesn't count. Only coming to work counts. Accept "I'll try" as a first step on the path to personal responsibility, then lock in a more robust commitment. Ask, "Will you do it?"

And avoid that seductive word "improve." For example, Susie was absent a total of 89 days last year; this year she missed 86 days. Has she improved? Of course, but she's a long way from acceptability. You don't want *improvement*. You want *correction*. In both conversations and documentation, *correction* is the operative term.

Managers can increase the probability that the employee will change and correct the attendance problem if they discuss the need for change in terms of the choices the employee makes. We each have the capability for choice; the coaching process turns that capability into reality.

It's always appropriate for the manager to think in advance about possible approaches or solutions the employee might use in attempting to resolve the attendance problem. But the responsibility for finding a solution to the problem is the employee's, not the manager's. If the manager makes a suggestion that the employee accepts and it subsequently turns out that the suggestion didn't work, look out! The employee will turn back to the manager and say, "See! I did what you told me and it didn't work!" So while the manager may assist the employee by making suggestions or offering guidance, the burden of actually solving the problem is always borne by the individual.

Good management practices need to be supported by tough-minded, straightforward policies. The best policy is also the easiest to install, maintain, and manage: If you come to work, you get paid. If you don't come to work, you don't get paid.

Period. That's it.

"Don't pay people for being sick," argues Arte Nathan, HR director for Las Vegas's Bellagio. The Bellagio, like Toyota of America and several other tough-minded organizations, has a forthright attendance policy: no work, no pay. Every employee is constantly exhorted to strive for perfect attendance and is rewarded richly for success. Toyota throws perfect-attendance parties where only those employees who have compiled perfect records are eligible to attend. Few eligibles miss the party—free Toyotas are given away. And the Bellagio also provides a jackpot for perfect attendance. Go six months without an absence, get a free day off. The Bellagio's perfect attendance percentage has risen from 51 percent to 68 percent since they inaugurated the program, Nathan claims.

Won't a policy like this encourage people to come in to work when they're sick? Of course it will, and so what, proponents ask. If an employee in one of these places ever challenges a supervisor who's discussing attendance by whining, "Well, you don't want me to come to work when I'm sick, do you?" the likely supervisory response is, "Yes, we do. We want every employee to be at work every day." This hard-line response is sometimes necessary with hard-line cases in any organization.

Installing a no-work, no-pay policy may be a little draconian for most organizations, but the message it sends is one that is appropriate anywhere: Coming to work is important, and each employee needs to take responsibility to arrange the conditions of his life so as to always be able to show up on time.

A less heavy-handed, but still highly effective approach is to change the focus of attendance control from the number of days or incidents of absence (an absolute value) to the individual's average absence rate (a relative value). Organizations that take this approach compute the average absence rate for the company as a whole or a specific department. Then they concentrate on those people whose attendance records are worse than average. The benefit of this approach is that it eliminates considerations of the cause of the absences. Instead, all the supervisor needs to say is, "The average absence rate in your department was 4.7 percent, Joe, but your personal absence rate was 5.5 percent." Even better, it gives the employee a reasonable target to shoot for. The supervisor can say, "We realize you can't be perfect, Joe. All we want you to do is be just a little bit better than average."

Joe only needs to put forth one percentage point's worth of improvement: move from 5.5 percent to 4.6 percent. But while he—and his often-absent colleagues—are getting slightly better, the average is moving, too. Other employees who were just under the line now become targets for talks about the need to do just a little bit better as their average absence rate goes over it. In a remarkably short period of time this average-based approach can move attendance problems from major crises to minor nuisances.

Absenteeism and the FMLA and ADA

Clearly, regular attendance is essential for most jobs, and you generally have the right to discipline, and even terminate, employees who do not meet your requirements. However, before you take action, you should consider whether an employee's absenteeism is related to medical conditions covered by either the Family and Medical Leave Act (FMLA) or the Americans with Disabilities Act (ADA). Both of these laws limit your right to discipline or discharge employees for attendance problems related to certain medical conditions. Find out what the laws, regulations, and courts have to say about this sticky subject.

FMLA Requirements

The FMLA requires covered employers to provide eligible employees with up to twelve weeks of unpaid, job-protected leave in any twelve-month period for certain family and medical reasons. In addition, you may not discriminate against employees who take FMLA leave. Therefore, you may not discharge or discipline employees for absences excused under its provisions, or take an employee's FMLA leave into account under "no fault" attendance policies.

So, for example, in *Thorson v. Gemini, Inc.* [205 F.3d 370 (8th Cir.), cert. denied, 531 U.S. 871 (2000)], the court found that the employer violated the FMLA when it terminated an employee for excessive absenteeism, defined as missing more that 5 percent of scheduled work hours, because the absences were covered under the FMLA. Similarly, in *Victorelli v. Shadyside Hospital* [128 F.3d 184 (3rd Cir. 1997)], the court determined that an employer may not discipline or terminate an employee for absenteeism that is the result of taking FMLA-protected leave.

Once employees have used up their twelve-week FMLA allotment, they are no longer protected by the FMLA, and you may take disciplinary action as a result of further absences. However, you still need to go further to determine whether the absences are protected by the ADA.

ADA Restrictions

The ADA can also affect your ability to discipline or discharge employees for excessive absenteeism that is related to a disability. The law requires covered employers to provide reasonable accommodations to qualified individuals with disabilities, unless doing so would impose an undue hardship on the business. Reasonable accommodations, depending on the circumstances, may include part-time or modified work schedules and unpaid leave. Thus for example, the Equal Employment Opportunity Commission's (EEOC) *Technical Assistance Manual* indicates that if an employee regularly needs a few hours off to obtain medical treatment for a disability, you should accommodate this need, unless doing so would impose an undue hardship.

The ADA, in effect, requires that these be considered "excused" absences or, in the case of no-fault attendance policies, that they not be counted for purposes of determining whether discipline is appropriate. In addition, you may have to accommodate disabled employees by allowing them to take more unpaid leave than is provided by your leave policy, unless this would impose an undue hardship.

If, however, a disabled employee is unable, even with reasonable accommodation, to achieve reasonably regular and predictable attendance, the employee may not be considered a qualified individual with a disability. Thus, his absences would not be protected by the ADA. So, for example, in *Wood v. Green* [323 F.3d 1309 (11th Cir. 2003)], the court ruled that an employee suffering from cluster headaches who requested indefinite leave so he could work at some uncertain point in the future was not a qualified individual under the ADA. It found that he could not perform the essential functions of the job presently or in the immediate future. And, in *EEOC v. Yellow Freight Sys.* [253 F.3d 943 (7th Cir. 2001)], the court determined that "in most instances, the ADA does not protect persons who have erratic, unexplained absences, even when those absences are a result of a disability," and that "attendance at the job site is a basic requirement of most jobs."

Some courts have found that regular and predictable attendance is not necessarily an essential function of all jobs. Thus, the court in *Ward v. Massachusetts Health Research Inst., Inc.* [209 F.3d 29 (1st Cir. 2000)], found little evidence in this case that a regular and predictable schedule was an essential function of a data-entry employee. It therefore ordered the employer to prove that the requested accommodation, an open-ended schedule, would create an undue hardship. In contrast, in *Earl v. Mervyns, Inc.* [207 F.3d 1361 (11th Cir. 2000)], the court concluded that punctuality was an essential function of a retail store area coordinator's job. It noted that the job required certain tasks to be performed daily at a specific time, that the employer placed heavy emphasis on punctuality as a business necessity, and that the employer had a progressive-disciplinary system for violation.

Actions to Prevent Liability

So, how do you make sure you are treating employee absences properly under the FMLA and ADA? Your best bet is to add the following extra steps to your decision-making process before you implement any disciplinary action:

1. Determine whether the employee has a medical condition that is protected under the FMLA or ADA. The FMLA covers employees with "serious health conditions," while the ADA only protects employees who have "disabilities."

2. If the employee is protected by either law, find out whether the absences are the result of the covered medical condition. Note that even if the employee is protected, if the absences are not caused by or related to the medical condition, you may take disciplinary action.

3. Impose disciplinary action only when the absences are not covered by the FMLA or ADA. In addition, if you do take disciplinary action, make sure you are acting consistently under your policies.

4. Check local laws. Many states have disability discrimination and family and medical leave laws that also limit discipline for absences.[1]

Finally, remember that FMLA doesn't apply in the great majority of problem-attendance cases. The biggest source of supervisory headaches is the occasional random unscheduled absence, and the Family and Medical Leave Act doesn't apply to those.

Courage is the primary requirement for effective attendance control. Too often supervisors hesitate taking on their truants because they doubt they'll be supported if the employee takes a complaint about supervisory heartlessness up the line. When the organization puts its policies in sync with its expressed desire to eliminate attendance problems, and when supervisors are backed up when they insist that people who get a paycheck show up to collect it, attendance problems can become a thing of the past.

Dealing with Attitude Problems

Harold Hook, the boy-wonder president of a couple of giant insurance companies, once opined that there are only three ways to make a basic, fundamental change in another person's attitude: deep psychotherapy, deep religious conversion, and brain surgery.

He may be right. The problem is, there isn't a manager around who's qualified to apply any of Hook's techniques. So put aside your concern about the attitude itself. Instead, concentrate on the specific behaviors that are sending your blood pressure into the stratosphere.

What's an "Attitude"?

Just what is an attitude anyway? When you think about it, all an attitude is, is a judgment that we make about a person based on what that individual says and does. It's the label we slap on another person's behavior when we don't like that behavior very much. But rather than using judgments and labels, the trick to solving attitude problems is to focus on what you know for sure—the specific things that the person did or said. You really never know for sure whether somebody's got a bad attitude. What you do know for sure is that two customers complained about being treated rudely.

"But it isn't just what he said," you argue, "it's the way he said it. It's his tone of voice, and facial expression, and mannerisms and demeanor." OK, let's agree that the cause of the tactless behavior really is some deep-seated attitudinal deficiency. What are you going to do about it? Our core attitudes are pretty well fixed by the time we're three. If you've got an employee who's got a shabby attitude because he was toilet-trained wrong at the age of two—or twelve—there's not much you can do about that now.

To start, when you feel the need to confront someone who's in need of an attitude adjustment, *never* use the word "attitude." It's futile. Any person with a genuinely vile attitude has probably had that fact pointed out to him so many times that he's anesthetized. Raising the attitude issue one more time will undoubtedly be unproductive.

Instead, narrow the problem down to specifics. What exactly is the person doing? Is he egotistical and credit-grabbing? Does she spend too much time socializing? Does he engage in pouting or sulking when he doesn't get his way? Or is she rude, surly, and inconsiderate? All of these behaviors are different, but all of them are commonly slapped with the "attitude problem" label.

Trying to fix "an attitude problem" without drilling down to the specific problem or exact concern is like shoveling smoke—a hopeless endeavor. So start by narrowing the issue to the specific problem or concern that's bugging you. Then write down the actual verbal and physical behaviors and actions that concern you—the evidence that the person is behaving in an unacceptable way. Be sure to record the nonverbals too—make note of rolling eyes, arms crossed tightly against chest, slow negative headshakes. Make believe you're a movie camera recording what you see.

Keep track of how often the behaviors occur. No one is *always* rude to customers; nobody *never* helps other team members when a project deadline approaches. Get your times, dates, and places exactly correct. This is a situation where keeping a log has a genuine payoff.

Once you've got an accurate and complete summary of a week or two's grating behaviors that have generated the "attitude problem" diagnosis, you're almost ready for a discussion. But not quite. You first need to answer the question, So what?

So what if the person behaves this way? What difference does it make? Your goal here is to be fully prepared to explain not only *what* the person is doing that causes concern, but *why* the situation must immediately be changed.

What is the impact of the individual's inappropriate behavior? What are the good business reasons why the organization expects employees to act in ways other than the way this guy's acting right now? What effect does the negative attitude have on customers and coworkers? How is the person's behavior at odds with the standards expressed in the company's statement of vision and values? What are all of the adverse effects of this individual's choice of behavior? Be ready to answer the "So what?" question in detail.

Addressing the Issue

With your written list of the unacceptable physical and verbal behaviors that you've observed, and the list of times and dates that they've occurred, and your summary of the good business reasons why an immediate correction must be made, you're fully prepared and ready to talk. Having this written list will enormously boost your self-confidence in raising the issue. Find a private place to talk. Discuss the situation with the individual and explain that his behavior—remember: his *behavior*, not his *attitude*—is causing a problem.

Here's the way to get your discussion off to a good start. Say, "Jack, I've got a problem and I need your help." Saying "I" instead of "you" reduces defensiveness. Then talk about the specific things you've seen and heard—the things you know for sure—that concern you. Tell the person exactly why they concern you, and then ask for the person's help in solving the problem.

Don't expect to get any useful responses. What you'll probably get is a lot of denial, and maybe even an accusation that you're paranoid. That's OK. It took this guy some time to get to you, you can take some time to get to him. So wrap up this initial discussion swiftly by saying, "That's great, Jack. I'm glad you feel there's nothing to it. Let's get back together in a week or so and just make sure that the problem's solved." Frequently, just finding out that others are aware of one's bad-boy behavior is enough to get people to decide to change.

A week later, if there hasn't been a total turnaround, talk again. Point out additional examples of inappropriate behaviors that concern you, and once more request a change in his ways. Again, expect denial, and again, wrap up the meeting on a positive note.

In all of these conversations, your job is to listen as much as it is to talk. Is there any reasonable explanation for the way the person is acting? Is Sally even aware of what she's doing? It may be that the inappropriate attitude is simply a coping mechanism for a genuine life challenge that the person is trying her best to contend with. This is where an employee assistance program is indispensable.

Raising the Stakes

If you need a third session, you now get more serious. Point out bluntly that getting along with others and maintaining cooperative and businesslike relationships are as much a part of the job as building widgets or processing insurance claims. People like this depend on the niceness of others to let them get away with their mischief. It's time to stop being nice.

Go over in detail the list of unacceptable behaviors you've observed. Describe exactly what the person did or said that was inappropriate. Review the time, the place, the reactions of others who were in the vicinity. Explain the good business reasons why change is mandatory—not preferred or requested, mind you, but obligatory and compulsory. Explain bluntly that the employee does not have a choice if he wants to keep his job. As the lawyers would put it, it is a *condition of employment*. And if you get a surly response of, "Well, that's not in my job description!" just grab his job description and write it in. Add a sentence that says, "The job incumbent will maintain a courteous, cheerful, and cooperative demeanor at all times, in spite of any personal problems or unpleasant customer behavior."

Too often, managers do a good job of identifying all of the manifestations of the attitude and the good business reasons why a change must occur, but they fail to come right out and straightforwardly say, "Stop!" Don't hesitate to tell the person that she must stop behaving in unacceptable ways. You're the boss; you set the rules. Tell the individual exactly what behavior is required: courteous, cooperative, and helpful.

Use Your Performance Appraisal Form

Your performance appraisal form can be a powerful tool in bringing about an attitude change, particularly if it's not performance appraisal time. Hopefully your appraisal form asks managers to assess not only the results the person produces, but their behaviors and competencies as well. Find the most appropriate place on the form to describe the person's attitudinal failings and write the narrative describing in detail the unacceptable behaviors. And be sure to circle the form's lowest rating, whether it's Unsatisfactory, or Fails to Meet Expectations, or a 1.

In the course of your conversation, hand the person the appraisal form and say, "Margie, I know it's not time for your performance appraisal right now, but if it were, this is what it would say." Then hand the damning (but accurate) appraisal to the individual and let her read the narrative and the rating. Then say, "Margie, unless there is a dramatic and sustained change in your interactions with coworkers and customers, this is what you can expect when appraisal time rolls around. I wanted you to see this now so there won't be any surprises."

When All Else Fails

In dealing with shabby attitudes, there are no guarantees. It may be that all your informal efforts fail and you have to move to formal disciplinary action and ultimately arrange a parting of the ways. But if you invariably demonstrate yourself the attitude you'd like to see in others, and have the courage to demand exemplary behavior as well as exemplary production, the odds go way up that that's what you'll get. And if termination does turn out to be the best answer, remember this: It's not the people you fire who make your life miserable. It's the people you don't.

Note

1. Information about FMLA and ADA reprinted with permission from HR Matters E-Tips, copyright Personnel Policy Service, Inc., Louisville, Ky. All rights reserved. www.ppspublishers.com.

The Administration of the Discipline System

Besides the inherent flaws of the traditional, punitive progressive-discipline system, there is another problem that causes this procedure to be an ineffective problem-solving tool: the way in which the system is administered.

Supervisors often hesitate to initiate disciplinary action not just because they don't like having to act in a punitive way, but because they don't know the answers to many of the questions that arise when the discipline procedure is begun:

- Whose permission do I have to get before I can hold a disciplinary transaction?
- Exactly how is it supposed to be documented?
- Who gets copies of the documentation?
- Should I ask the employee to sign a copy?
- How long does it stay in effect?
- Is the employee allowed to request a transfer?
- Is he allowed to appeal?

Whatever system an organization uses, these administrative issues must be resolved for supervisors to feel confident that they are taking appropriate action. More important, these issues must be resolved if the management of the enterprise is going to feel confident that disciplinary discussions are being held appropriately, consistently, and within the guidelines of company policy.

In this chapter we identify and address every major administrative issue that must be resolved for any system of disciplinary action to work. We review the alternatives available, the benefits and limitations of each, and the decisions that organizations that have implemented the Discipline Without Punishment system have made. Even for organizations that plan no change to the formal steps of their current approach, a review and updating of their current administrative procedures can greatly increase the effectiveness of the system.

As Figure 10-1 illustrates, the complete Discipline Without Punishment system has a total of six individual elements, including the three formal steps of disciplinary action.

Some administrative questions or issues may not apply directly to every element shown in Figure 10-1. For example, "Maximum number allowed?" is irrelevant when termination is the element under consideration; "Appealable through the Grievance Procedure?" is rarely a concern with regard to Positive Contacts. Still it is helpful to make sure that all administrative aspects are considered for each element of the system.

The Elements of Administration

Initiator

• *Issue: Who should be the person responsible for initiating the action in question?*

Almost without exception, every organization feels that the immediate supervisor (at whatever level) is the person who bears the responsibility for initiating each element of Discipline Without Punishment. Making anyone other than the direct supervisor responsible for initiat-

Figure 10-1. The Discipline Without Punishment system.

INFORMAL TRANSACTIONS

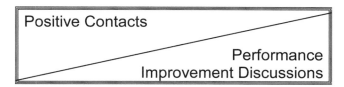

Positive Contacts

Performance
Improvement Discussions

FORMAL DISCIPLINARY
TRANSACTIONS

FIRST	Reminder 1
SECOND	Reminder 2
FINAL	Decision Making Leave

TERMINATION

Termination

ing action reduces supervisory authority. By holding the immediate supervisor responsible, the organization reinforces the importance of the first-line supervisor's job.

In some companies it is not always clear who an individual's "immediate supervisor" is, particularly when matrix structures or self-directed work teams or working foremen (nonmanagement employees who provide work direction and handle administrative details) are used. The best way to resolve the issue is to determine who would be responsible for giving the individual a performance appraisal and salary increase. That same person is probably the most appropriate candidate to handle any disciplinary transactions required.

Prior Approval

• *Issue: Whose approval must be gained before the planned action can be taken?*

No organization requires the immediate supervisor to gain anyone else's approval before conducting a Positive Contact or a Performance Improvement Discussion. These are considered regular, on-going elements of any supervisor's job.

Some organizations allow supervisors to conduct a Reminder 1 discussion without the prior approval of anyone else in the organization. Other companies, particularly those whose supervisors have not had much experience or formal management training, require them to get approval from their immediate supervisor or department head before taking this step. Most organizations encourage supervisors to review their plans to begin formal disciplinary action with the human resources department, but few formally require HR's approval at the Reminder 1 level.

Almost all organizations require the immediate supervisor to get approval from both the department head and HR before conducting a Reminder 2 discussion.

At the Decision Making Leave and termination steps, most organizations require that these actions be approved in advance by the department head, a senior HR manager, and a member of senior management.

Location

• *Issue: Where should the meeting be held?*

The critical requirement is that the location be somewhere private—and on-premises: Don't hold a disciplinary discussion over a cup of coffee at Starbucks.

Witness Required?

• *Issue: Is a management witness required to be present during the conversation with the employee?*

No organization requires a management witness to be present for

Performance Improvement Discussions or Positive Contact discussions. Few require a witness in order for the supervisor to conduct a Reminder 1 transaction. Many require a witness at the Reminder 2 stage, and almost all organizations require a management witness to be present when an employee is placed on a Decision Making Leave or terminated.

In every case where a witness is present, however, the organization expects the immediate supervisor to be the initiator of the transaction and to conduct the discussion. The witness's role is simply to be "a witness."

In unionized organizations, the employee's union representative must be present at the time any disciplinary discussion is conducted, or at the time that the employee is involved in the investigation of a situation that could possibly lead to disciplinary action. Few nonunion organizations allow employees to bring in a witness or representative to the meeting, except in the rare cases where language differences require the need for a translator.

Documentation

- *Issue*: *How will the action be formally documented once it has been taken?*

The documentation procedures for Performance Improvement Discussions and the three formal steps of the Discipline Without Punishment system are covered in full in the chapters on those steps (Chapters 5 and 6). Positive Contacts are typically documented with an informal note to the employee or, if the employee's action was particularly meritorious, with a formal memo to the individual with copies to senior management.

Terminations can be documented with a summary memo to the file with a complete chronological listing of all the events that led up to the termination. All documents relating to previous disciplinary action should be collected and filed with this summary memo.

Employee Signature

- *Issue*: *Should the employee be required to sign the documentation to acknowledge receipt?*

As I explained earlier, there are many benefits to not requiring the employee to sign a copy of the documentation memo until the Decision Making Leave, the final step of the system.

Distribution

• *Issue*: *Who gets copies of the documentation? Where will the records be held?*

Records of Positive Contacts, Performance Improvement Discussions, and Reminder 1s are usually kept in the departmental file, not in the employee's permanent personnel record. Many attorneys, however, advise that there should only be one real personnel file and encourage organizations not to maintain any form of personnel records within the department.

For Reminder 2s and Decision Making Leaves, the original of the memo documenting the discussion goes to the employee; the supervisor who wrote the memo retains a copy. Other copies of the memo are sent to the department head and the HR department for inclusion in the employee's official records. Additional copies of the memo, particularly at the Decision Making Leave step, may be sent to other senior managers, particularly if they were involved in approving that action. All documentation regarding termination is kept with the rest of the former employee's records.

Length of Time Active

• *Issue*: *If the employee improves his performance, corrects the problem, and maintains satisfactory performance for a significant period of time, should he have the right to have his slate wiped clean?*

Most organizations agree that allowing the employee to get disciplinary action deactivated after the problem has been corrected is a good idea, particularly since the chance to purge one's file of detrimental information is a significant incentive for improvement. Few, however, have developed workable procedures for "deactivating" disciplinary action.

In the course of implementing Discipline Without Punishment, organizations begin by first coming to agreement that they will establish a formal mechanism for deactivating disciplinary action. They then must decide how long each step will stay in effect. Most decide that the time frames should vary, with initial steps being deactivated quickly and later steps remaining active for a longer period of time.

The matrix shown in Figure 10-2 reflects the range of decisions that companies that have implemented Discipline Without Punishment have made regarding the length of time a step will remain active.

Most organizations decide to deactivate the disciplinary action in the same way that it was activated. In other words, if the Reminder 2 step was formally documented with a memo to the employee with copies to the department head and the personnel file, it seems reasonable to deactivate the action with a similar memo with copies distributed to the same recipients. The memo should recognize the individual for correcting the problem and maintaining the improvement over a significant period of time.

There may be exceptional situations that require special provisions. For example, an airline that was implementing the Discipline Without Punishment system encountered a major obstacle when the time frames for deactivation were being determined. While all of the managers involved in the implementation were comfortable with a recommendation that Reminder 2s would remain active for six months and Decision Making Leaves for one full year, the vice president of Flight Operations was adamant that any disciplinary offense committed by a pilot that affected operational safety remain active forever. The company ended up adopting a policy that provided for the six month/twelve month time frame, supplemented by a footnote that specified that any issues that dealt specifically with flight safety would be decided on an ad-hoc basis.

Figure 10-2. Active duration of Discipline Without Punishment steps.

Step	Shortest Time Period	Longest Time Period
Reminder 1	3 months	12 months
Reminder 2	6 months	18 months
Decision Making Leave	9 months	24 months

What should be done with the memo documenting the disciplinary action that was placed in the individual's personnel file? Most companies remove it from the individual's file and place it in a separate "Dead Disciplinary Action" file on a chronological or alphabetical basis. In this way the employee's future prospects will not be compromised long after a problem has been resolved by retaining an antiquated disciplinary notice in the personnel file, yet the record will still be available if needed to demonstrate organizational consistency in actions taken with others.

Responsibility for Notification

•   *Issue*: *Whose job is it to remember when the active period has expired?*

The employee is responsible for keeping track. At the time of the incident the employee should be advised of how long the disciplinary action will remain active, and told that it's his responsibility to notify his supervisor when the guideline period has expired. The supervisor will then notify HR to move the documentation to a "dead disciplinary action" file.

When Can Steps Be Repeated?

•   *Issue*: *How many Reminder 1s or Reminder 2s may a person receive before moving to the next more serious level?*

Every organization provides that a person may receive an unlimited number of Positive Contacts and Performance Improvement Discussions.

Almost all allow an employee to receive more than one Reminder 1. The caveat, however, is that they must be given for unrelated problems.

As described earlier, all disciplinary problems fall neatly into one of three mutually exclusive categories: attendance, performance, and conduct. Most organizations with Discipline Without Punishment allow an individual to receive two or even three Reminder 1s, provided that they result from problems in different categories. Thus a person who received a Reminder 1 for above-average absenteeism (an issue in the attendance category) might receive a second Reminder 1 for failing to meet a deadline (a performance issue, unrelated to attendance). However, the same individual would usually be given a Reminder 2 if a problem of tardiness arose after the initial Reminder 1 for above-average absences. While tardiness was not exactly the same offense, it falls into the same category: attendance.

Organizations often decide to allow a person to receive more than one Reminder 2, again provided that the problems triggering the action are in different categories. However, every organization considers the Decision Making Leave to be a singular event. Since the employee is required to make a commitment to totally acceptable performance in every area of his job, there is little justification for allowing the step to be repeated.

When Can Steps Be Skipped?

• *Issue: When an individual commits a serious disciplinary infraction, can early steps be skipped and a Reminder 2 or Decision Making Leave step be taken directly? What are the situations that justify termination for a first offense?*

Throughout this book we have assumed that when problems arise, they arise at a level of seriousness that the manager begins by considering training or job engineering interventions. If these initial approaches do not work, then the manager proceeds, in order, through holding a Performance Improvement Discussion and then the steps of the Discipline Without Punishment procedure. While this assumption is valid for the majority of problems that arise, there are offenses so serious that training or coaching or even a Reminder 1 is inappropriate. And there are rare cases where termination is appropriate even for a first offense.

The most manageable way to separate the lower level offenses from the more serious ones is to assign all disciplinary problems into one of three categories: Level 1 (minor), Level 2 (serious), and Level 3 (major).

Level 1 problems, the great majority, are those relatively minor issues that do not involve honesty or trust, do not by themselves constitute a threat to the operation of the business, and pose no threat to the safety or well-being of employees. Excessive tardiness, poor housekeeping, overstaying breaks, and other minor inefficiencies are examples of problems at this level of seriousness. For these problems, if training and Performance Improvement Discussions are not sufficient to bring about a change, the discipline process would begin with the Reminder 1 and continue through the remaining steps.

Level 2 issues are serious offenses that constitute some degree of threat to the operation of the business or to the safety of employees. These may include violations like smoking in a room where oxygen is in use, gambling on company property, showing up for to work in unfit condition, reporting a false reason for an absence, or being absent without notification. For these offenses, either a Reminder 2 or a Decision Making Leave would be considered appropriate by most companies. The final decision would depend on the actual seriousness of the violation, the employee's work record, the action the company had previously taken in similar cases, and the supervisor's best judgment about which step would be the more effective in solving the problem.

Finally, there are *Level 3* violations. These are major offenses that seriously threaten the operation of the business or the safety of employees, or demonstrate, in and of themselves, that the offender has so little personal integrity and self-esteem that his continued presence cannot be tolerated. Deliberate falsification of records, theft and fraud, assaulting a supervisor or coworker or customer, selling drugs on the premises, and possession of firearms are almost always considered major offenses.

Discharge is the appropriate remedy for major offenses. However, it is important that the employee never be discharged at the time of the incident. If the employee is terminated in the heat of the moment, he is almost sure to be returned to work if the termination is later challenged. The arbitrator or hearing officer or judge will determine that in spite of the employee's actions, the company responded without conducting any investigation or letting cooler heads prevail.

Still, immediate action is required in these cases. Use the phrase, "You are suspended pending investigation," at the time of the incident and remove the individual from the premises. Once the employee has left (and it may be necessary to call security or the police), the company can make a full investigation and determine if there are any mitigating circumstances that would preclude the decision to terminate. Even when the violation is flagrant and the facts are clear, it is only to the organization's benefit to wait until the following day to make the termination decision official. In this way, if the action is ever challenged later, the company can testify truthfully that at the time of the incident the individual was not terminated but was relieved of duty and suspended pending investigation. After sleeping on it overnight and seeking in vain for any mitigating circumstance, the company made a sober and objective decision to terminate.

This type of suspension, called "crisis suspension," is not a part of the formal discipline process. It is an emergency action taken to allow the organization the time required to determine which element of the Discipline Without Punishment system is appropriate. The time the employee spends away from work on a crisis suspension is normally without pay, unless the investigation concludes that the suspension was unjustified.

In short: There is no offense that an employee can commit that justifies "termination on the spot."

Is the Action Appealable?

• *Issue: Can the individual appeal the action through an existing internal dispute resolution procedure (e.g., open door policy, Peer Review procedure, or internal grievance system)?*

Employees who are represented by a union will automatically have access to a formal grievance procedure that provides for the complaint ultimately to be heard and resolved by an outside arbitrator. Non-union organizations that have "open-door" policies typically allow employees who feel that disciplinary action or discharge actions were inappropriate to appeal them to the president or another senior officer. While few open-door policies provide any genuine due-process protections for the employee, they may suggest some semblance of organizational fairness.

While appeal procedures are inappropriate for Positive Contacts or Performance Improvement Discussions, most companies allow employees to use any available appeal mechanisms for any step of the discipline process.

Maximum Performance Appraisal Rating

• *Issue*: *If an employee is on an active step of disciplinary action, is there a limit on how high a rating he can get on his performance appraisal?*

There have been many cases of people getting an "Exceeds Expectations" rating on their annual performance review in spite of the fact that they received a formal step of disciplinary action only a month or two before. To prevent this, some organizations provide that an individual may not receive any rating higher than the middle category of their rating scale until the disciplinary action is no longer active.

Eligibility for Transfer?

• *Issue: If the company has a job-bidding procedure whereby employees can request a transfer to another job, is an individual allowed to request transfer while he is on an active step of disciplinary action?*

Some companies prohibit the use of their job bidding or transfer request procedure until an employee successfully completes the active period of any disciplinary step, believing that a person should correct his problem and be at a minimally acceptable level of performance before being allowed to request a transfer to a different department. Others allow an employee on a Remainder 1 to use the transfer request system but prohibit its use at more serious levels. Most prohibit employee-initiated transfers during the active period of a Decision Making Leave.

Such restrictions, of course, do not apply to any company-initiated transfer or promotion. The organization can always decide to transfer or promote an individual, even though that person may be on an active step of the Discipline Without Punishment procedure.

If an employee is allowed to transfer, however, such action never affects the active period of the disciplinary action.

Eligibility for Compensation Change?

•   *Issue: If the individual becomes eligible for a compensation change while on an active step of the discipline procedure, (e.g., cost of living increase, annual salary adjustment, merit increase) will the increase be granted or will it be deferred/delayed/denied until the action is no longer active?*

If an automatic, across-the-board compensation change is granted to all organization members, there is little justification to withholding this change from those individuals who are currently on an active step of disciplinary action. The only criterion for receiving this type of salary or wage adjustment is simply being on the company's payroll.

But if an employee becomes eligible for a merit increase or other individually determined compensation adjustment while he is on an active step of disciplinary action, should the increase be granted? Several possibilities exist:

1. Grant the increase and take no account of the fact that the individual is on an active step of discipline.
2. Grant the increase but reduce the amount to reflect the seriousness of the disciplinary action.
3. Delay the increase until the disciplinary action becomes inactive, then grant the full amount of the increase retroactive to the date on which the employee became eligible.
4. Delay the increase until the disciplinary action becomes inactive, then grant the increase effective on the date on which the disciplinary action became deactivated.

Of these four possibilities, the one that is probably the easiest to manage and to justify to the individual is number 4. Most organizations feel that it makes little sense to take a step that places an individual in jeopardy of ultimately losing his job, and then turn around and send an entirely contradictory message by awarding that person a "merit" increase.

Discipline During the "Probationary Period"

Most organizations decide that the formal Discipline Without Punishment system will not apply during the employee's initial employment or "probationary" period. They believe that access to the discipline system is an employee benefit that the employee earns by demonstrating sufficient self-discipline to become a member of the regular work force.

It is reasonable for a manager to assume that the performance, behavior, and attendance that he sees during the initial employment period is the finest that the employee is capable of. If a performance problem arises with a new employee that would be serious enough to warrant a Performance Improvement Discussion with a regular employee, the manager should hold a very serious discussion with the individual and consider whether the new employee is properly suited for this job at this company. If the problem continues, or if a problem serious enough to warrant a formal disciplinary conversation arises at any time during the initial employment period, the most appropriate response is termination.

The Policy Matrix

In the course of resolving the basic policy and procedural issues involved in an implementation of the Discipline Without Punishment system, many companies create a "policy matrix." This document provides, on a single page, complete administrative guidelines, and it is of immense value to supervisors.

In Appendix E, you will find an actual matrix created by one organization as part of its implementation of Discipline Without Punishment. While the decisions represented on this matrix would not be appropriate for all organizations, they are reasonable and appropriate for their culture, history, and organizational mission.

CHAPTER 11

Creating a Discipline Without Punishment System

Individual managers can achieve a great deal of personal success by applying the techniques of dealing with people in a nonpunitive way. However, an organization-wide implementation of Discipline Without Punishment (DWP) involves a major cultural change effort. Formal policies and informal day-to-day practices must be reviewed and reconsidered. Supervisors need to be trained in the new approach, the belief system behind it, and the techniques for holding nonpunitive disciplinary discussions. Management must communicate to everyone concerned the purpose of the system, the reason for the change, the specific administrative practices, and the commitment of senior executives to this new approach.

Discipline Without Punishment must also be linked with all other existing human resource policies and programs: performance appraisal, attendance management, grievance and appeal mechanisms, employee assistance programs. The training provided managers must be synchronized with other training and management development efforts so that all development efforts are seen as integral parts of an overall strategy and not as merely another "program-of-the-month."

Finally, after installing the new program, managers must measure, monitor, and maintain it.

For more than a quarter century I have helped some of America's best managed organizations install the Discipline Without Punishment system. As a result, I have developed a straightforward and consistent implementation process that any company can follow. In this chapter I describe the implementation procedure as it would apply to a large organization with several organizational units and a large number of employees—perhaps a thousand or so. For smaller organizations the process will be easier, faster, cheaper, and simpler. But large or small, three critical factors will determine whether the Discipline Without Punishment implementation will be successful: the development of suitable policies and procedures, the training of all managers, and the creation of organization-wide understanding, support, and acceptance.

Where to Begin

The decision to implement a Discipline Without Punishment system usually begins when one individual in the organization becomes aware that there is an alternative to traditional ways of handling disciplinary problems. Whether that person is a line manager or a member of the HR function, implementation begins with illumination—a light dawns in one person's mind that a better way exists.

From this point the idea of making a change to the discipline system must be sold within the organization. Since replacing the organization's current system for handling matters of discipline with the Discipline Without Punishment approach is a matter of policy, the company's policy-making officials must be involved in the decision.

Although the agreement of senior management can be obtained through meetings with individual executives and the building of support one-on-one, a more rapid and effective strategy is to conduct an "executive overview" of the approach for a group of key line and staff managers, once the organization's curiosity has been tweaked. The purpose of this meeting is not to decide to implement Discipline

Without Punishment; it is, rather, to give everyone concerned enough information to decide whether Discipline Without Punishment is an approach that is consistent with the values and culture of the organization. If the executive overview is approached more as an educational and exploratory opportunity than a marketing and decision-making session, the chances for favorable consideration rise.

The Executive Overview Agenda

Successful executive overviews share two common characteristics: They provide full information on the rationale and mechanics of the Discipline Without Punishment approach, and they demonstrate that the organization will benefit from adopting the system based on history and current conditions within the organization.

Information on the operation of Discipline Without Punishment can be obtained from this book as well as from the experience of other organizations that are using the approach successfully. Managers will want answers to such questions as:

- What types of companies are using the approach?
- Why is a nonpunitive system more appropriate for our company, our people, and our managers than what we are doing now?
- What benefits are we likely to gain?
- What administrative issues will need to be resolved?
- How do the policies and practices of Discipline Without Punishment compare with what we're doing now?
- What kind of implementation process will be required for our organization? How long will it take? Who needs to be involved?
- How will we know that the new system is successful?
- How much will it cost, both directly and indirectly, to implement Discipline Without Punishment?

Current data from inside the organization itself can be used to demonstrate the need for an approach that emphasizes commitment

and personal responsibility and eliminates punishment. Begin by looking for data on how well the current system is working:

- How many disciplinary incidents occurred in the last year?
- How serious were these incidents—how many verbal reprimands, how many suspensions, and so forth.
- What kinds of problems caused disciplinary action to be taken?
- How many people resolved the problem following a disciplinary conversation? How many moved on to the next step?
- How many people were terminated? How many of these termina- tions were grieved or otherwise challenged?

Whereas these data will be useful in demonstrating the need, few
organizations have the monitoring and tracking systems in place that
allow this information to be easily captured. Fortunately, problems
with the existing system usually are not the major impetus for an organization's changing to a nonpunitive approach.

The primary reason that organizations make the change is not because their current system isn't working well. It is because, whether it
is working well or poorly, the underlying adversarial philosophy and
punitive mentality don't fit the values and vision of the organization.
Most organizations use the traditional discipline system not because
they embrace its values and assumptions about people, but because
they don't know another way.

There are actually very few organizations that scrap their current
practices and move to a nonpunitive approach because their existing
system is provoking the same kind of hostility and resentment that
prevailed in the Frito-Lay plant that caused the approach to be created. Companies are moving to Discipline Without Punishment
because they have outgrown the assumptions that underlie the traditional approach. What they have done for years no longer fits.

Creating Organizational Ownership

When organizational change efforts fail, the primary reason is rarely a
deficiency in the new system or program itself. Most of the time failure
results from a lack of ownership.

To assure success there must be shared ownership on the part of everyone who has a stake in the system's success. The best way to assure the successful implementation of Discipline Without Punishment is to create an Implementation Team and charge it with the responsibility of tailoring the system and assuring a smooth transition from the organization's current practices to the Discipline Without Punishment approach. Among the tasks to be accomplished by this team are these:

• Establish the degree of management authority at each level of the system.
• Clarify the specific roles and responsibilities of line management, HR, and top management.
• Develop procedures for deactivating disciplinary action when an employee has successfully solved a problem.
• Determine the severity of various infractions.
• Develop effective documentation procedures.
• Identify any unique training needs.
• Link Discipline Without Punishment and all other related performance management programs.
• Develop organization-wide understanding and support.

This Implementation Team is a task force of anywhere from a half-dozen individuals in a small organization to as many as two dozen in a large firm with many divisions. They come from different functions in the organization and different levels of management. Members are almost always exempt, management-level employees—from first line supervisors up to senior operating officers, including specialized individual contributors like a representative from the corporate counsel's office and HR and training specialists.

While a few companies have successfully included nonmanagement employees on the Implementation Team, virtually none have invited union representatives to participate in the development of the system. In spite of the productive relationship that many companies enjoy with their union and their view that including the union president or business agent on the Implementation Team will enhance that relationship, I recommend against it.

Here's why: Several years ago I was managing the implementation of Discipline Without Punishment with a large oil company in Houston. The company had worked for several years to develop a partnership relationship with the union and we all anticipated we could further that goal by including the local union president and a shop steward on the team. Our plan worked reasonably well until the day that the Implementation Team was assessing the seriousness levels of different infractions: What were Level 1 offenses, which were Level 2 offenses, and what would be considered Level 3 offenses—major violations that called for termination for a first offense?

In the middle of our discussion, the union president called a recess. He said that he and the shop steward needed to be excused from service on the Implementation Team. "We really can't participate in this," he explained. "If we agree that sleeping on the job is a major offense, then we've really compromised our ability to process a grievance for a member who might get terminated for sleeping. You guys need to make those decisions by yourself."

He was right, of course. The job of management is to make the rules; the union's responsibility is to make sure that management plays by the rules it has made. If those roles are compromised, then both sides suffer and the employee himself will surely be the loser.

A corollary is that in most cases management does have the right to implement the Discipline Without Punishment approach unilaterally without negotiating the change with the union. Several arbitrations have upheld the right of management to implement any discipline system it wanted provided that it met reasonable tests of fair play and due process. Unions have the right to grieve any action taken under that system if it is inconsistent, excessive, or otherwise unfair. Only in situations where the specific steps of the traditional progressive-discipline system are codified in the union contract does management have to negotiate the change with the union, and this can usually be accomplished by a joint letter of agreement. Few unions have raised any real objection to the elimination of warnings and unpaid suspen-

sions; most have accepted the change with a note of "skeptical acceptance."

Unions find little to complain about in the theory of Discipline
Without Punishment, but are often suspicious about whether managers will actually walk the talk. Several unions, in fact, have been active
proponents of the system, in some cases bringing the approach to
management's attention directly and recommending that the company consider installing it.

The Duties of the Implementation Team

The Implementation Team's first responsibility is to understand the
system as fully as possible. This can be accomplished by providing the
team members with a shortened version of the training program in
which all managers will ultimately participate.

Their second responsibility is to concentrate on one of two primary areas: developing appropriate policies and procedures, and assuring understanding and support. If the Implementation Team is large
(a dozen people or more), it's useful to subdivide it into two task
forces, each with a different agenda: policy and communications.

The mission of the *policy* task force is to draft a Discipline Without
Punishment policy statement and come up with procedural guidelines
for initial approval by the Implementation Team as a whole and final
approval by the organization's senior management. It is also charged
with the responsibility to develop the procedures needed to measure,
monitor, and maintain Discipline Without Punishment once it has
been installed.

The other task force concentrates on *communications*. Its members function as a specialized advertising agency. Their "product" is
their company's proprietary Discipline Without Punishment system
that their counterparts on the policy task force are creating. Their
market is everyone in the organization who might be affected by the
system. And their mission is to develop a communications plan that
will assure complete understanding, support, and acceptance by all.

The Policy Task Force

The specific issues that will be addressed by the policy task force are:

- To whom does DWP apply?
- How many formal levels of discipline may an individual receive?
- How long will formal levels of discipline remain active?
- What will "deactivation" involve?
- Who must approve at each level of the procedure?
- Will employees on an active step of disciplinary action be eligible for promotion? Transfer? Compensation change?
- When can steps be skipped? When can they be repeated?
- How will crisis situations be handled?
- What other systems and procedures (attendance, performance appraisal, compensation, employee assistance, etc.) will need to be integrated with DWP?
- What will be the status of employees who are on an active step of disciplinary action at the time DWP is implemented?
- What will be the documentation requirements?

And there will be more issues that will come up as the policy task force works on tailoring the Discipline Without Punishment system to the specific needs and culture and history of its company.

The Communications Task Force

The communications task force faces a similarly demanding assignment in addressing the following issues:

- How will we position DWP—a completely new program, part of our on-going efforts, a gradual change, or a major change?
- What communication has taken place so far?
- What rumors are circulating about DWP and/or the decision to implement it?

- What should be the timing, frequency, and method of communication?
- What misunderstandings about DWP are likely to arise? How can we avoid and correct these misperceptions?
- Who are all of the interested parties or stakeholders? What information about DWP do they need?
- What is the appropriate role of senior management:
  - During the implementation process?
  - During the training program?
  - After the formal implementation date?
- What needs to be included in the management training program to make it specifically appropriate for our organization?
- What information do nonsupervisory employees need?

In a large organization, the Implementation Team's work usually takes between six and twelve weeks, depending on the availability of members to meet regularly and to complete individual assignments between meetings. In most cases, the individual policy and communications task forces will have two or three working sessions between each full meeting of the whole Implementation Team. Task force meetings usually last one to three hours as participants deal with specific issues and wrestle with the various approaches and recommendations. The meetings of the entire Implementation Team are usually scheduled for a full day.

While the number of meetings of the Implementation Team will vary from one organization to another, as a rule of thumb it is worthwhile to estimate that there will be three meetings, each of which will consume most of a full day. The agenda for these meetings is as follows:

Implementation Team Meeting #1

- Develop a common understanding of the Discipline Without Punishment system and philosophy.

- Begin development of Implementation Team members as internal performance management consultants.
- Assign Implementation Team members to the policy and communications task forces.
- Develop project timetable and goals.
- Identify key issues to be resolved over the course of the project.
- Identify any immediate communication requirements.

Implementation Team Meeting #2

- Review/revise/approve initial policy and procedure recommendations.
- Identify any remaining or unanswered policy issues for further policy task force review and recommendations.
- Review/revise/approve overall communications plan.
- Review plans and provide feedback on the format, media, and content for management training and employee communication sessions.

Implementation Team Meeting #3

- Review, discuss, and approve any remaining procedural recommendations and the policy matrix.
- Review and provide feedback on the final draft of the policy.
- Review and approve final plans for employee communications.
- Review plans for management training programs.
- Review/revise/approve transition plans.
- Finalize all remaining decisions and activities prior to training.

There is also usually a final meeting of the Implementation Team immediately after the last management training seminar. During the training programs, participants will have raised questions and made suggestions about the program. This collection of questions and suggested additions and deletions produced by seminar participants is circulated to all Implementation Team members. Each item is reviewed and deliberated. The team makes its final decisions about any changes to the final draft policy that had earlier been approved by the executive group. It completes work on any other pieces of business that were either left over from the previous team meeting or arose during the management seminars, including the plans for monitoring and maintaining the system after implementation.

At this point, the work of the Implementation Team is almost entirely completed. The only remaining major activity is conducting the employee communications sessions, the communications task force's final duty.

When possible, it is appropriate for the Implementation Team members to meet with the senior management group, both to make their recommendations on any final modifications to the draft policy and procedures, and to be recognized by the organization's executive group for their success in arranging the transition to the new approach.

Management Training

The management training seminar to implement the Discipline Without Punishment program usually consumes a full day—seven to eight hours of training. In addition to gaining the skills necessary to handle one of the most difficult parts of their jobs effectively, managers must also understand and accept the new philosophy that underlies the procedures they are learning and the new skills they are acquiring. Even with a skilled trainer and an enthusiastic audience, the task of transferring all of the knowledge, attitudes, and skills is challenging.

The objectives for the training sessions are straightforward. By the end of the workshop, each participant needs to be able to:

1. Conduct effective "Positive Contact" discussions and use recognition to encourage good performance.
2. Describe the difference between desired performance and actual performance in a specific and objective manner, without using generalities, judgments, or concerns about "attitude."

3. Explain the good business reasons why a performance problem must be solved and the logical consequences that will follow if the situation is not corrected.

4. Conduct effective discussions with employees about the need for performance improvement that result in the employee's agreement to change.

5. Document all transactions—both informal Performance Improvement Discussions and formal disciplinary transactions—quickly, confidently, and accurately.

6. Be able to conduct a disciplinary discussion at each level of the Discipline Without Punishment procedure (Reminder 1, Reminder 2, Decision Making Leave) properly and confidently.

7. Be able to handle the everyday problems of attendance, tardiness, and "bad attitude."

8. Be able to explain all procedural issues involved in the company's procedures, including approval levels, length of time various actions are active, documentation requirements, deactivation requirements, and so on.

9. Be able to answer common questions from employees about the system and explain why the organization has decided to invest in this program.

10. Understand, accept, and enthusiastically support the nonpunitive philosophy of the program.

The actual content of the seminar will vary greatly, based on the needs of the organization and its previous management development efforts. The greatest chunk of seminar time, however, needs to be spent having managers actually practice holding effective discussions with subordinates. Other major topics to which most organizations choose to devote a great deal of time include recognition of good performance, the review of the final drafts of the policy and procedural guidelines (including the solicitation of recommendations to the Implementation Team), and a discussion of the requirements needed to make the transition to the new system successful.

But Where's the Pound of Flesh?

Besides giving managers the skills to handle people problems effectively, a constant if subtle objective of the management seminar is to develop acceptance of the nonpunitive philosophy on the part of all participants. Old ways die hard. Both in convincing senior managers to adopt the Discipline Without Punishment system and in convincing managers to give up their old ways and deal with troublemakers with dignity and grace, a lot of emotional resistance must often be overcome.

When the City of Arlington, Texas, was considering implementing Discipline Without Punishment for all city employees, its HR director engaged me to conduct an executive overview. Around the conference table sat the senior management group: the city manager and a deputy, the city attorney, the head of HR, and two or three other senior operating officials.

As I explained the operation of the system, the reasons other organizations had implemented it, and the results they had achieved, the city attorney showed more and more signs of distress. While it was obvious that he fully understood and appreciated the logical and rational reasons why Discipline Without Punishment was a better way of dealing with people than the approach that they had used for years, his heart just wasn't in it. The logic was clear; but an emotional barrier was preventing his accepting the approach.

He challenged me with one abrasive question after another: What about this, how would you handle that? Would you ever suspend a person without pay for a week or two if the steps of the Discipline Without Punishment approach failed to convince him to change? No, I responded, once a person has been through all the steps of Discipline Without Punishment and continues to perform unacceptably, termination's the appropriate response. Isn't it true that some people change as a result of punishment? Yes, that's true, I replied. But implementing Discipline Without Punishment reflects an organization's decision to eliminate punishment as a way of managing people, even though a few people may respond better to being punished than to being forced to take personal responsibility for their own behavior.

Finally, even though all of his questions had been answered and the logic of the system was apparent, he was still unconvinced. He shook his head, then looked direct'y at me and blurted out, "But where's the pound of flesh?"

At that moment I realized that he had identified the biggest obstacle that managers must overcome in order to accept a nonpunitive approach to handling disciplinary action: There is no pound of flesh.

No benefit comes without its price. I had always considered Discipline Without Punishment to be an approach that was cost-free, except for the direct dollars and time invested by the organization to install the approach. But that city attorney had identified a very real cost that I had never considered: the cost of giving up the ability to "settle the score" with someone who had misbehaved.

The city attorney had put his finger on a rarely admitted but deeply felt need of many managers: to respond in kind to inappropriate organizational behavior. When an employee misbehaves, comes to work late, or confronts citizens or customers with a hostile attitude and a chip on the shoulder, a manager often wants more than simply a correction of the problem and a commitment to future good performance. *Often he wants revenge.*

Giving up this deep-seated, visceral need to settle the score is the price managers have to pay for implementing Discipline Without Punishment. They get improved performance and a deeper commitment to the organization and its expectations, but they don't get revenge. You give up the ability to gain the emotional satisfaction of settling the score. And sometimes that's not enough. What we really want is that pound of flesh. It can take every ounce of maturity that we've got to turn loose of our need for revenge and be satisfied merely with solved problems and enhanced relationships.

Building Management Commitment

The management training seminar to implement the Discipline Without Punishment system usually closes by having participants anticipate their transition back to the workplace and the way in which they will explain the Discipline Without Punishment system when they are asked about it, as most of them will be. Working in teams they identify the most difficult, most embarrassing, most disconcerting questions they feel they might be asked by their employees when they return to their workplaces. Some of the questions they anticipate having to answer deal with the procedural mechanics of the Discipline Without Punishment system (How many Reminder 2s can I get, or, What if I get sick on my Decision Making Leave day?) Most, however, concern far more substantive issues. The great majority of the questions they identify usually reveal issues that they may not yet have fully resolved for themselves:

- At a time when the company is talking about the need to cut costs, why are we investing so much money in a program like this?
- Isn't this just a quicker way to get rid of people?
- I never create any disciplinary problems. What's in this for me?
- I've seen lots of programs come and go. Isn't this going to be just another good idea that gets off to a big start and then fades away and is forgotten?
- Why do we need to have a discipline system, anyway?
- These new steps are just the same old thing with new names. There's nothing really new here, is there?
- I like what you say about recognizing those people who do a good job, but do you really think that's going to happen?
- What will happen to a manager who doesn't follow this program, who keeps on acting like he's always acted? And what about the manager who sees people doing their jobs wrong and goofing off and doesn't say anything about it . . . will anything happen to them?

Each team then answers the questions thrown at them from the others. When participants discover that they are able to answer whatever question they are asked convincingly and forthrightly, they also discover that they have incorporated the essence of Discipline Without Punishment. They may not know all of the mechanics, and they will soon forget many of the specific details. But their subordinates are not usually concerned with testing the boss to see if he can remember everything that he was taught in charm school. What subordinates really want to know from those to whom they look for leadership is, what do you think about this? Are you really committed to it? Do you believe that this will really make a difference and make this a better place for me to work?

Once the manager discovers that she is fully capable of answering that question, not from her head but from her heart, it is time to close the proceedings and send the participants on their way. The seminar has done its job.

Moving Toward Implementation

Once all of the organization's supervisors and managers have completed the management seminar, the Implementation Team meets for its final session. The agenda for this session is to resolve all of the questions and issues that were raised by the participants in the management seminars.

The issues brought up to the Implementation Team range from the most mundane—a typographical error, an obvious miswording—to substantive matters that require genuine discussion and provoke difficult decisions. If there have been several management training seminars, as there invariably are in large organizations, it is important that at least one Implementation Team member be present in every one. By sprinkling Implementation Team members throughout the seminars, they can share with their colleagues the rationale the team used in arriving at the many procedural decisions that it made. Equally important, they can bring back to the team a full explanation of any of their colleagues' concerns or recommendations.

The ideal close for the final Implementation Team meeting is a presentation by team members to the organization's executive leadership concerning the final policy recommendations and implementation plans. The official date for the start of the new program will be confirmed, and the plans for monitoring and measuring the results will be reviewed. Finally, team members will be recognized for their efforts in creating the system.

Three more major activities must still take place before the official implementation date of the system:

1. An executive orientation session
2. The employee orientation program
3. Individual notification to employees who are on an active step of disciplinary action under the old system of their status once the new system goes into effect

Executive Orientation

One concern invariably raised by participants in the management seminars involves whether top management will actually support the efforts of lower-level managers who use the system well and make the tough calls required for any discipline procedure to work right. While they may not have personally experienced the situation, they have all heard horror stories of supervisors who accumulated a great store of documentation of an individual's continuing failure to meet organizational standards, only to be rebuked and reversed in their attempt to gain approval to terminate. Even though the factual content of many of these stories varies widely when closely checked out, managers still perceive upper management as being unsympathetic to the day-to-day employee problems they have to deal with.

It would be nice if the entire senior management group would fully participate in each management seminar as regular enrollees and not as a short-time, drop-in observers. However, because the needs of top executives are sufficiently different from the needs of middle managers and supervisors for whom the management seminar is designed, their inability to be regular participants is not a significant obstacle to program success. Senior managers almost never conduct disciplinary discussions.

What senior managers do need to do is to coach middle managers and supervisors on their expectations of high organizational performance and their insistence that all of the techniques and procedures and skills acquired in the seminar be used as presented.

Instead of attending the management seminar, a more effective and convenient approach is to schedule an executive orientation program of about two hours, typically conducted by a combination of the facilitator for the training programs, the Discipline Without Punishment project manager, and the chairman of the Implementation Team. The objectives of this session, tailored to meet the specific needs of the individuals represented in the executive group, include enabling them to do the following:

- Understand completely all of the policy and procedural elements of the organization's proprietary Discipline Without Punishment program as tailored and modified by the Implementation Team.

- Understand the importance of and accept the responsibility for:

  - Using the appropriate terminology (i.e., never referring to a Reminder 1 as a "verbal reprimand").

  - Using all elements of the system in their personal performance management actions.

  - Holding subordinate managers accountable for using and administering the system correctly.

- Coach their subordinate managers in their attempts to use the system properly.

- Recognize when subordinate managers are using the Discipline Without Punishment system properly, and recognize and reinforce their activities appropriately.

- Recognize when subordinate managers are not using the Discipline Without Punishment system properly, and provide the necessary coaching and other corrective action to change their use of the program.

- Understand, accept, and enthusiastically support the nonpunitive nature of the organization's "Discipline Without Punishment" philosophy.

Employee Orientation Program

For most of an organization's employees, the only contact they will directly have with the Discipline Without Punishment system is when their conscientious performance is recognized in a Positive Contact or similar transaction. They will be affected indirectly by the system when they discover that their poorer performing colleagues are confronted with the need for change, and the few who do not accept that responsibility disappear.

They will be able to tell that the system is working when they sense that morale around the place is higher. They will know that things are different when their supervisors give them specific directions and more useful feedback, instead of merely saying "Do your best," or "Try harder."

But they will probably not be aware of the intimate mechanics of the Discipline Without Punishment procedure since they will never be recipients of any of the formal levels of the discipline system. However, it is important that all members of the organization be familiarized with the entire procedure since one of the great benefits of the approach is the peace of mind that it provides to all organization members. In case they ever do become embroiled in a disciplinary scrape they know that they will be dealt with with dignity, that they will have the chance to emerge from it with their pride intact, and that, ultimately, they will have the chance to have their record cleansed.

For this reason, most organizations schedule a series of orientation programs to introduce all employees to the overall Discipline Without Punishment procedure. By this time there have been several announcements and updates produced by the communications task force over the course of the implementation process. This session is the major communications vehicle to assure organization-wide understanding of the approach and the reasons for adopting it.

Some organizations choose to make the implementation of the Discipline Without Punishment system a major event. They may produce a videotape that explains the company's rationale for moving away from an adversarial approach and into a system that focuses on decision making and personal responsibility. The steps of the system are usually reviewed in detail and the company's commitment to recognizing good performance is emphasized. Some companies use outside narrators and actors and engage professional producers (or make use of their own equivalent internal resources) to produce a broadcast-quality production.

Other lower-budget approaches can be just as effective. A large chemical company, in spite of abundant resources, chose a simpler approach. They put a single camera on a tripod and pointed it at the senior operating manager, a man of tremendous integrity and internal credibility. He stood next to a flimsy flip chart on which he had personally written some of the core concepts of Discipline Without Punishment. The camera recorded him as he talked simply and directly, telling every member of the organization why he had decided to adopt this system and why he believed in it. He expressed his bone-deep conviction that once every person out there got familiar with it, they would believe in it just as strongly as he did. It was a performance that no amount of Hollywood slick could make any more credible.

Whether highlighted by a superb video production, or just a simple meeting led by the members of the Implementation Team, the objectives for the employee orientation program are the same. By the end of this one-hour session, each employee should understand:

- The reasons that the organization chose to implement a program that emphasizes decision making and personal responsibility.
- The mechanics of each element of the company's Discipline Without Punishment system (Positive Contact, Performance Improvement Discussion, Reminder 1, Reminder 2, Decision Making Leave).
- The specific personal benefits in the new system (the "What's in it for me?" question).
- How Discipline Without Punishment integrates with other organizational efforts to improve the culture and quality of work life.

Individual Meetings

Shortly before the system's official implementation date, individual meetings need to be held with each person who has received a formal disciplinary transaction during the last year or so. Each of these individuals is advised what decision has been made about where he or she stands under the new system.

Deciding on transition procedures is another important responsibility for the Implementation Team. From the moment that the organization decides to install Discipline Without Punishment and begins the implementation process, detailed records should be kept of every disciplinary transaction that occurs. In addition, a search of the records should be made to identify all members of the organization who have received disciplinary action in the recent past so that all cases can be considered in moving to the new approach. While the organization may not have had a formal "active period" under the previous system, every person who has received a formal disciplinary transaction in the past year or two will remember that fact and will be concerned about what his status will be once the new system goes in place.

There are three alternatives available to the Implementation Team in deciding what to do about individuals who are on active disciplinary steps at the time of transition to the new system. First, they can wipe the slate clean for everyone (everybody gets a fresh start). Second, they can reduce each discipline step one level (an active Written Warning under the old system becomes an active Reminder 1 once the new system is installed). A third alternative is to maintain everyone under the new system at the same place they were under the old (a person with an active written warning under the old system now is considered to be on an active Reminder 2).

Implementation Teams usually begin the decision-making process by determining how many people are on active steps of disciplinary action, who these people are, and at what level in the system they are. If there is a reasonably small number of individuals and they are not clustered at the final level of disciplinary action, then it would be a major gesture of good faith on the organization's part to wipe the slate clean for everybody. The experience of most organizations that have elected to wipe slates clean universally is that there is little correlation between the people who get their slates wiped clean and those who get into disciplinary scrapes following the new system's inauguration.

If there is a larger number of individuals on active disciplinary steps, if these individuals are clustered at the more serious end of the disciplinary action scale, and if there are a couple of genuine trouble-makers for whom it would be a serious error to allow them to return to a clean slate, the approach of "everybody take one step back" makes sense.

In this situation there would be no one who enters the system at the Decision Making Leave level, even if an individual had previously received more than one suspension. Anyone who was previously at a final-step level would now be at the Reminder 2 stage and eligible for a Decision Making Leave if a disciplinary problem arose again. Those who had previously received a written warning would now be considered to be at the Reminder 1 stage.

While it might be possible, it would be unwise to move individuals lockstep from a step of the former system to the equivalent step of the new Discipline Without Punishment procedure. It is doubtful, too, whether any arbitrator or other third party could be convinced of the appropriateness of that decision. Even organizations that absolutely insist on personal responsibility and decision making find a place for mercy. This is the place.

Once the decision about how the transition will be handled has been made by the Implementation Team and approved by senior management, it becomes the responsibility of individual supervisors to advise each of their subordinates who are on active discipline steps what their status will be at the time of the new system's inauguration. The Implementation Team, assisted by the HR function, usually prepares a script for the supervisor to follow, telling the employee what his current status is and communicating the supervisor's expectation that the employee will never again commit any disciplinary offense. This message is particularly important when the company has generously decided to let bygones be bygones and provide a fresh start for all.

Choosing an Implementation Date

Frankly, the date itself makes little difference.

No matter how long the Implementation Team spends in developing the policies and procedures, the timing of the overall project is not particularly critical until the management training programs begin. It is desirable to have all management seminars scheduled as closely as possible. Several organizations have used teams of trainers and scheduled management training sessions concurrently so that all the training could be done in the shortest possible period.

Once the final management training program has been completed, the amount of energy in the organization for moving into the new system will be at a peak. It would be a mistake to allow this energy to dissipate by unduly delaying the actual start date of the program. In the seminars, managers will ask about when they can start using the procedures. They should be told to start using their new skills and the new procedures immediately. The "Implementation Date" is not the *first* day on which the new system goes into effect; it is, rather, the *last* day on which any of the elements of the old progressive-discipline system can be used.

As soon as the final management seminar has been conducted, the following events must occur:

- All recommendations and suggestions from the participants in the management seminars must be collected, organized, and circulated for review to all members of the Implementation Team.
- The Implementation Team must hold its final meeting and resolve each issue coming out of the management seminars, including transition plans and the development of a system to measure and maintain the Discipline Without Punishment program once it goes into effect.
- The recommendations of the Implementation Team, plus the final drafts of all policy statements and procedural elements of the system must be approved by senior management.
- The executive orientation program must be scheduled and conducted.
- The employee orientation programs must be scheduled and conducted.
- All administrative materials and forms must be printed and circulated.

- Each employee on an active step of discipline under the previous system must be advised of his status under the new system.

Measuring the Effectiveness of Discipline Without Punishment

As soon as implementation day arrives, the system for monitoring and maintaining the system goes into effect. During the previous months of work by the Implementation Team, they should have been collecting as much data as possible on the activities and effectiveness of the old system so that they can use it as a basis of comparison with the new.

There are three aspects that an effective measurement plan considers: the nature and amount of activity that occurs under the new system; the reactions and perceptions of organizational members; and the operating and human resource results that can be attributed to the system.

The determination of what to measure should be made in conjunction with the senior management team, taking into account the ease with which data can be collected and the resources available to devote to the measurement effort. What will senior management accept as evidence that the system is working effectively? A reduction in the number of disciplinary incidents may not be a true measure of success if the organization was previously managed so loosely that anything less than a physical assault was met with little more than a dark glance and the admonition to "knock it off."

For most organizations, however, a reduction in disciplinary action is a mark of success. A better indicator could be a reduction in the number of people who proceed from one level to a more serious level. Almost always, a reduction in discharges is beneficial (although the reverse may be true for organizations that previously provided assurance of lifetime tenure regardless of performance or behavior.)

Tracking all of the data on the amount and type of disciplinary activity, particularly the number of Positive Contacts and Performance Improvement Discussions, will not only provide an indicator of system use but also highlight those sections or departments that are experiencing significantly more or less activity than other organizational units. Whether this is good or bad will require direct investigation, but locating potential problem areas will be greatly facilitated.

It may be particularly important to measure the number of official Positive Contact transactions. One of the primary reasons organizations decide to implement the Discipline Without Punishment system is to move toward an environment where good performance is frequently recognized and reinforced. After an initial flurry, supervisors often fail to maintain their good intentions of regularly recognizing good performance. But if they are required to report the number of transactions they have had on a quarterly basis, for example, there is an added incentive to continue what they know they should be doing anyway.

Besides simply counting the number of incidents of each element in the system, another important area to measure is the reaction of organization members to the system. How do they feel about it? Would they go back to the old way?

Either as part of the initial implementation process, or as an early activity in the management seminars, many organizations conduct a survey to determine the reaction of organization members to the company's current performance management activities. If designed properly, this same survey can be re-administered six months or a year after installation to see whether the perceptions of people have changed. Questions covering these areas are reasonably easy to construct and respond to using a "1 to 5" or similar scale:

- Are people whose performance is unacceptable confronted with the need to change?
- Are people whose performance is above average recognized for their contributions?
- Do managers feel confident in their ability to hold productive disciplinary or coaching discussions?
- When a supervisor recommends termination, does senior management usually support the recommendation?

- Is the amount of paperwork required by the system excessive?
- Is the relationship between nonmanagement employees and company managers pleasant, professional, and respectful?

In addition to specifically constructed surveys, any existing employee attitude data can provide valuable information about the perceptions of organization members in the area of how their performance is measured.

Managing and Maintaining Discipline Without Punishment

"We're up to 35,000 feet at 625 knots," the copilot told the captain of the 747. "We can turn the engines off now."

You can't turn the engines off, even after Discipline Without Punishment is fully launched and flying high. Systems fail not because they weren't well designed or well implemented. Systems fail for two reasons: no ownership and poor maintenance.

We have dealt with the ownership issue by using an Implementation Team to create the policies and procedures, and by not making the policy official until all managers were given the chance to propose revisions. Making sure that the system is continually well maintained helps guarantee that initial success will continue.

But from the first day of implementation the system will begin to deteriorate. Supervisors, who were experts on holding effective coaching conversations and disciplinary transactions at the end of the seminar, find that their skills rapidly atrophy when they are not frequently used. Managers who could answer any question about policy administration the day after the seminar are hard pressed to respond when a month has gone by. New supervisors join the organization to replace departees; Implementation Team members move on. As attention to the system necessarily becomes reduced in the weeks and months and years following the rush of energy that accompanies implementation, plans must be drafted and carried out to assure that skills and awareness are maintained at high levels. The employee handbook must be revised to incorporate information about the approach. The employee orientation program needs a section to let new employees know that, should performance problems ever develop, they can expect to be treated differently here than they would be in a less desirable place to work.

As the supervisory population changes, plans for a repetition of the original training program for new supervisors and refresher training for existing supervisors must be made and carried out. The videotapes, posters, and booklets that may have been prepared to explain the program at the beginning should not gather dust in the closet forever.

At some point, however, an organization's reduction in high-profile attention to Discipline Without Punishment ceases to be a matter of concern. This apathy occurs when the system is imperceptibly transformed from a mere "program" and becomes a fully integrated aspect of life in the organization.

As part of my research for the original edition of this book and almost two decades after I had developed the Discipline Without Punishment approach at Frito-Lay, I returned to the company to find out whether the system was still in place. While I had maintained close relationships with many Frito-Lay colleagues in the years since I had left the company to begin my consulting practice, I had never been back in any professional capacity. In the twenty years since then that I have been helping organizations develop their own nonpunitive systems based on the work I had first done at Frito-Lay, I had always been able to make the confident statement, "No company that I have ever worked with to implement Discipline Without Punishment has ever abandoned it." I wanted to be able to continue to say that.

Frankly, I was nervous when I drove into corporate headquarters to talk with Terry Taillard, the corporate director of training and development, the same job I had when Discipline Without Punishment was born. I had good reason to be nervous. When I called Taillard earlier to ask about Frito-Lay's current use of Discipline Without Punishment, he confessed that he wasn't familiar with a program by that name.

I met Taillard in the cafeteria. As we sat by a window overlooking the handsome grounds of what many consider to be the most beautiful corporate campus in America, my anxiety disappeared when he explained his earlier statement about being completely unfamiliar with anything called "Discipline Without Punishment." "Oh, we use it everywhere in the company," he told me. "I just didn't know it had a name. It's just the way we do business here."

*   *   *

The final test of the effectiveness and success of Discipline Without Punishment is when it stops being a program . . . a project . . . a policy. Discipline Without Punishment is finally and fully implemented when it has become so incorporated into the grain of organizational life that everyone considers it "just the way we do business here."

Discussion Worksheet: Pre-Meeting Checklist

Name of Employee: _____ Date: _____

Supervisor: _____

Type of Problem: ❑ Attendance   ❑ Performance   ❑ Conduct

Dates of any previous discussions about the problem: _____

_____

Basic Issue / Overall Concern: _____

_____

_____

Desired Performance: _____

_____

_____

_____

Actual Performance: _____

_____

_____

_____

Impact: (The good business reasons why the problem must be solved) _____

_____

_____

Consequences: (The logical consequences the individual will face if he or she fails to correct the situation) _____

_____

_____

The Five Classic Questions:

- ❑ Did the employee clearly understand the rule or policy that was violated?
- ❑ Did the employee know in advance that such conduct would be subject to disciplinary action?
- ❑ Was the rule violated reasonably related to the safe, efficient, and orderly operation of the business?
- ❑ Is there substantial evidence that the employee actually did violate the rule?
- ❑ Is the action planned reasonably related to the seriousness of the offense, to the employee's record with the organization, and to action taken with other employees who have committed a similar offense?

Action (This discussion is intended to be):

- ❑ Performance Improvement Discussion   ❑ Reminder 1
- ❑ Reminder 2   ❑ Decision Making Leave

Discussion Worksheet:
Post-Meeting Summary

Employee Name: _____

Discussion Date: _____

**Gaining
Agreement:** Did the employee agree to solve the problem / correct
the situation? ❑ Yes ❑ No

Notification: Was the employee advised of the specific action
taken (Performance Improvement Discussion,
Reminder 1, Reminder 2, Decision Making Leave)?
❑ Yes ❑ No

**Employee
Assistance
Program:** Was the employee provided information / referral to
the EAP? ❑ Yes ❑ No

Summary of discussion: _____

_____

_____

_____

_____

Employee's solution (Action the employee will take to correct the situation): _____

_____

_____

_____

_____

Other solutions (Action to be taken by yourself or other people to help the employee solve the problem):

_____

_____

_____

Employee's reaction (Summary of employee's comments about the situation or the discussion):

_____

_____

_____

Completed by: _____

Follow-up date: _____

Sample Memo: Reminder 2

MEMORANDUM

To: Myra Thayer

From: Albert Hall

Date: April 30

Subject: Reminder 2

CC: John Webber, Production Manager
            Ellie Laurel, Personnel

Earlier today you and I met with John Webber to discuss your performance. I explained that this was a serious matter and that, because we had talked about your need to improve your performance several times in the past, we were issuing a formal Reminder 2.

The basic problem, Myra, is that while you do an excellent job in the actual selling part of your job, your performance is unacceptable in all of the support areas that are also part of your job requirements. Some of the examples we discussed include these:

1. About two weeks ago a customer returned a pair of hiking shoes that she had purchased three weeks before. While you could have processed the return and credit yourself, you told the customer that she would have to go to customer service in order to have the transaction completed. The customer reported to one of the customer service representatives that you had said you were too busy to take of the return when it appeared you were not busy at all.
2. You have been consistently late in sending your Record of Inventory summary to the accounting office.
3. When you are working the end of day schedule, you frequently leave merchandise in the wrong places and fail to leave your unit in such condition that the person working the start of day shift can immediately begin work the next morning.

When you and I had our last conversation about this problem on February 22, at which time I issued you a Reminder 1, you said that you understood the need to handle all parts of your job as effectively as you handle the selling part. Unfortunately, that has not happened, and the problems we talked about earlier continue.

Myra, this situation is serious and must be immediately corrected. The failure to do so will lead to more serious disciplinary action and could result in your discharge from the company. As John and I explained during the meeting, no matter how good your sales are, if you cannot meet all of the job requirements we will be unable to keep you as an associate of the company.

I know that you can do as good a job in meeting the administrative and merchandising requirements as you do in meeting our selling expectations. You agreed that you would, and I look forward to your putting this problem behind you.

s/ Albert Hall

Sample Memo: Decision Making Leave

Memorandum

To: Gerri Borland

From: Robert Quadro

Date: June 29

Subject: Decision Making Leave

CC: Cyril Burt, Production Manager
Cecile Nostramus, Vice President—Operations
Julie Hewitt, Vice President—Human Resources

You were placed on a Decision Making Leave on June 28 because of your failure to perform and record all safety checks before certifying that the equipment for which you were responsible was ready for shipment.

245

This problem was initially brought to your attention in several informal discussions you and I had earlier this year. When the problem continued, you received a formal Reminder 1, the first step of our discipline procedure, on April 21. Later, on May 14, you received a Reminder 2, the second step of our discipline procedure.

In each of these conversations I reviewed exactly what our expectations were, and you agreed that you would follow them. When the same problem arose earlier this week I reviewed the situation with Mr. Burt, Ms. Nostramus, and Ms. Hewitt, and we agreed that a Decision Making Leave, the final step of our discipline policy, was appropriate.

I advised you that this was the final step of our discipline procedure and that you were to make a final decision—either to solve the problem of performing and recording all safety checks and, in addition, to commit to fully acceptable performance in every area of your job, or to quit. When you returned from the Leave you told me that you wanted to continue your employment and that you would solve the problem and would perform every part of your job in a fully acceptable manner.

As I advised you during our meeting, you must immediately correct this situation. In addition, you must maintain fully acceptable performance in every area of your job, whether related to this issue or not, since any further problems that require disciplinary action will result in your termination.

s/ Robert Quadro

Sample Policy Matrix

[Name of Organization]
[Name of Program]

ACTION / Issue	Initiator	Prior Approval	Location	Management Witness Required?	Documentation Required	Employee Signature Required?	Documentation Distribution	Maximum Number Allowed	Length of Time Active	Responsibility for Notification	Appealable?	Maximum Performance Appraisal Rating	Eligible to Request Transfer?	Eligible for Compensation Change?
POSITIVE CONTACT	Supervisor and above	None	Anywhere	Encouraged	Encouraged	N/A	Departmental Employee File (if memo)	Unlimited	N/A	N/A	N/A	N/A	Yes	Yes
INFORMAL DISCUSSIONS														
INFORMAL COACHING	Immediate supervisor	None	Anywhere private	No	None	N/A	N/A	Unlimited	N/A	N/A	N/A	N/A	Yes	Yes
PERFORMANCE IMPROVEMENT DISCUSSION	Immediate supervisor	None	Anywhere private	No	Performance Discussion Worksheet (memo optional)	No	Departmental File	Unlimited	N/A	N/A	No	N/A	Yes	Yes
FORMAL DISCIPLINE LEVELS														
REMINDER 1	Immediate Supervisor	None	Anywhere private	No	Performance Discussion Worksheet	No	Departmental File	3	6 months	Employee	Yes	Superior	Yes	Yes
REMINDER 2	Immediate supervisor	Dept. Manager	Manager's Office	Dept. Manager	DWP and memo to employee	No	Departmental File and Personnel File	2	12 months	Employee	Yes	Fully Successful	Yes	No
DECISION MAKING LEAVE	Immediate Supervisor	Dept. Mgr. and HR Rep.	Manager's Office	Dept. Manager and HR Rep.	DWP and memo to employee	Yes	Departmental File and Personnel File	1	18 months	Employee	Yes	Needs Improvement	No	No
TERMINATION														
TERMINATION	Immediate Supervisor	Dept. Mgr. and HR Mgr.	Manager's Office or HR	Dept. Manager and HR Mgr.	Letter of Separation and Status Change	No	All records to HR	N/A	N/A	N/A	Yes	N/A	N/A	N/A

SAMPLE PERFORMANCE MANAGEMENT MATRIX

Index

About the Author

Dick Grote is Chairman and CEO of Grote Consulting Corporation in Dallas, Texas. He is the developer of the GroteApproach[(SM)] Web-based performance management system, and the author of *Discipline Without Punishment* and *The Complete Guide to Performance Appraisal*, both published by AMACOM. Both books were major book club selections and have been translated into Chinese and Arabic. His most recent AMACOM book was *The Performance Appraisal Question and Answer Book*.

Paramount Pictures bought the movie rights to the original edition of *Discipline Without Punishment* and produced the award-winning video series "Respect and Responsibility" with Dick as host. His latest book is *Forced Ranking: Making Performance Management Work*, published in 2005 by the Harvard Business School Press.

Dick Grote's articles and essays have appeared in the *Harvard Business Review*, the *Wall Street Journal*, *Across the Board*, and over two dozen other business and general interest magazines and journals, including *Cosmopolitan*. For five years he was a commentator on life in the workplace for National Public Radio's *Morning Edition* program. For over twenty years he was adjunct professor of management at the University of Dallas Graduate School.

In college, Dick was a member of Colgate University's retired undefeated GE College Quiz Bowl Team. At 63 he still competes regularly in 5K and 10K races (occasionally bringing home a third-place trophy).